WALKING ORDERLY,

KEEPING THE LAW

A PRONOMIAN
POCKET GUIDE TO
ACTS 21:20-26

G. SCOTT MCKENZIE

Walking Orderly, Keeping the Law: A Pronomian Pocket Guide to Acts 21:20-26

Copyright © 2024 G. Scott McKenzie. All rights reserved.

Pronomian Publishing LLC
Clover, SC 29710

ISBN: 979-8-9908630-1-9

WALKING ORDERLY,

KEEPING THE LAW

A PRONOMIAN
POCKET GUIDE TO
ACTS 21:20-26

G. SCOTT MCKENZIE

In memory of my Dad (Greg "Bo" McKenzie).

There was a drop of water that once landed on a placid lake, and that is all it took to shake the world.

CONTENTS

INTRODUCTION

Should Christians keep the Law of Moses? Did the apostles teach that the Torah was abolished or that Christians, especially Gentiles, should transition away from it? For most of historical Christianity, the Post-Torah paradigm has ruled the day, stretching all the way back to the divisions between Rome and Asia-Minor in the second century AD.[1] However, this is beginning to change. Over the past several decades (though I would argue that Torah-continuity has been defended since Paul wrote his letter to the Galatians), an increasing number of scholars have shown that antinomianism cannot remain internally consistent or cohesive. Law-free theologies fail to correspond with historical and grammatical realities, and most importantly, they cannot adequately account for overtly pronomian texts like Acts 21.

Indeed, Acts 21 presents a significant hermeneutical challenge for all antinomian theologies. In this text, James dismisses accusations

---

[1] Post-Torah, as defined by Tim Hegg, refers to the era of the believing communities (churches) in which the primary matrix of "faith and practice" is entirely without connection to the Torah. Hegg compares the term Post-Torah to Postmodernism in that, in the postmodern era, life is seemingly lived without concrete truth. Tim Hegg, "All Things to All Men: Paul and the Torah in 1 Cor. 9:19-23, Torah Resource. https://tr-pdf. s3-us-west- 2.amazonaws.com/articles/all-things-to-all-men.pdf (Date Accessed July 23, 2023).

that Paul taught against the Law, affirming instead that Paul "walk[ed] orderly, keeping the Law" (Acts 21:24). The challenge for antinomian readings of Paul is reconciling Paul's supposed antinomianism with the Jerusalem elders' conclusion that Paul was indeed upholding the Torah in his teachings throughout Asia Minor. Accordingly, two primary theories have emerged within Christian theology to address this tension (see below). However, I will argue that these theories do not sufficiently explain Acts 21 or Christ's words in Matthew 5:17-20.[2]

To accomplish the task at hand, this book is divided into chapters that cover the primary objections to a Pronomian reading of Acts 21:

- Chapter 1 presents a logical argument based on the biblical text. I argue that Paul is either a liar, a madman, or a truth-teller.
- Chapter 2 delves into the methodology and arguments of what is known as the "Transitory Theory." This chapter likewise demonstrates that the biblical narrative and certain antinomian proof-texts (Acts 15; 20:6-7, Rom. 14, Col. 2, and the Resurrection accounts) are unable to substantiate a transition away from the Law of God.
- Chapter 3 investigates the most common Evangelical objection and their reason for thinking that Gentiles have a "Law-free option" in orthopraxy, which is what I have termed the "Conciliatory Theory." Accordingly, this chapter includes a review of 1 Corinthians 9 and what it means to be "all things to all men."

---

2   For an excellent overview of Matthew 5:17-20, see David Wilber, *How Jesus Fulfilled the Law: A Pronomian Pocket Guide to Matthew 5:17-20* (Pronomian Publishing, 2024).

- Chapter 4 addresses other arguments that are typically presented as an answer to Acts 21, including the "Civil, Ceremonial, Moral" distinction and whether or not Paul's actions at the Second Jerusalem council are a matter of doctrinal indifference.
- Chapter 5 concludes this book by demonstrating that Acts 21 serves as a hermeneutical key for Pauline rhetoric.

I hope this short book gives you greater insight into how the apostles walked orderly and kept the Law.

CHAPTER 1

EITHER PAUL OR A BAD MAN

C.S. Lewis pioneered an argument for the authenticity of the claim that Christ is the Son of God. The crux of his dilemma is that either Jesus was telling the truth or that he was a madman or even the devil himself.[1] In Lewis's *The Lion, the Witch, and the Wardrobe*, Prof. Diggory Kirke helps Peter and Susan determine that their sister Lucy is neither a lunatic nor a liar by bluntly asking them a series of questions regarding Lucy's record of behavior, especially in comparison to their brother Edmond's. They come to the only logical conclusion, which is that Lucy was in fact telling the truth.[2] This argument has become known in Latin as *aut Deus aut malus homo* (either God or a bad man). Despite this argument's seeming imprecision and oversimplicity, it holds water and deserves its storied success as one of Lewis's most popular apologetic arguments for the divinity of Jesus (Yeshua).[3]

It was the simplicity of this argument and its relationship to bibliology that spurred the idea that it might be applied as a hermeneutical "logic test" to the writings and actions of the apostles, most notably John, James, Paul, and Peter (the apostolic pillars for both Jerusalem councils—Acts 15 and 21). These men were certainly not perfect or

---

1   C.S. Lewis, *Mere Christianity* (Harper Collins, 2001), 53; "Christian Apologetics," in *God in the Dock: Essays on Theology and Ethics*, ed. Walter Hooper (Eerdmans, 2001), 101; "What Are We to Make of Jesus Christ?" in *God in the Dock*, 167-168; "Rejoinder to Dr. Pittenger," in *God in the Dock*, 196; See also G.K Chesterton, *The Everlasting Man* (Hodder and Stoughton, 1926), 191-210.

2   C.S. Lewis, *The Lion, the Witch, and the Wardrobe* (Harper Collins, 2000), 47-51.

3   David A. Horner, "Aut Deus aut Malus Homo: A Defense of C.S. Lewis's 'Shocking Alternative," in *C.S. Lewis as Philosopher: Truth, Goodness, and Beauty*, 2nd ed, eds., David Baggett, Gary R. Habermas, and Jerry L. Walls (Liberty University Press, 2017).

divine; in fact, it was because of Peter's violation of his own direct instruction from the Lord (Acts 10 and 11) that he stood condemned by Paul in Galatians 2:11-12. But given that the instructions handed down by the apostles in Acts 15 and 21 are doctrinally binding and inspired Scripture, it stands to reason that the apostles can also be tested by Lewis's dilemma. Were the apostles lying (or insane) or were they truthful? It is a basic logical hermeneutics test.

Acts 21:21-24 is the main text at hand:

> ...and they have been told about you, that you are teaching all the Jews who are among the Gentiles to forsake Moses, telling them not to circumcise their children nor walk according to the customs. What, then, *is to be done?*[4] They will certainly hear that you have come. Therefore do this that we tell you. We have four men who are under a vow; take them and purify yourself along with them, and pay their expenses so that they may shave their heads; and all will know that there is nothing to the things which they have been told about you, but that you yourself also walk orderly, keeping the Law.
> —Acts 21:21-24

What seems to have escaped real scrutiny is the actual logic of this text. There are only two options for what Paul was preaching in the

---

4   *"to be done?"* is italicized in the NASB 95 and indicates that the ἐστιν is "implied" and not in the original Greek. But I believe that James's original question stands on its own, "What then is!?" As will become clear, it seems that James is rather surprised by the news that he and Peter have heard about Paul's preaching. It seems to be a question as to Paul's real actions in the diaspora. James is simply asking Paul if these accusations are true. The KJV simply, and correctly, states, "What is it therefore?", which is speaking directly to the charge of apostasy instead of what Paul and James should do.

diaspora: either Paul was preaching the forsaking of Moses, or Paul was not preaching the forsaking of Moses. Interestingly, Paul's words are not recorded by Luke in this exchange with James. However, what is recorded is the insistence that Paul *is not* preaching the forsaking of Moses to the Jews in the diaspora, which is shown by James' imperative to partake in what is probably a Nazirite vow to show that Paul "walks orderly, keeping the Law."[5] Given this fact, the reader can only arrive at one of three possible conclusions to interpret this text:

1. Paul is telling the truth.
2. Paul is lying to James.
3. Paul is a madman.

Therefore, *aut Paulos aut malus homo*. Either Paul is a truthful man, or he is a bad man and ought to be abandoned as a false apostle.

James's Fact-Finding Mission, the Context, a Very Serious Charge, and the Birth of a Theological Conundrum

Before continuing, as is the case with all hermeneutical efforts, a basic contextual grammatical overview is in order, especially given the seriousness of the charges against Paul in the logical analysis of Acts 21. From the total context of Acts 21, it is clear that both Jews and Gentiles were coming to faith in Messiah in some rather large numbers. James says in v. 20 that "many thousands" among the Jews located in Jerusalem have believed. The word that is translated "many thousands," *myriads*, is at a minimum ten thousand and up to "an innumerable host." Perhaps even a translation of ten thousand times

---

5   See Num. 6:1-21 for the requirements of the Nazirite vow: purification, refraining from grapes and wine, sacrifices, and shaving of hair.

ten thousands is appropriate. The typical understanding regarding the Jews of the first century, according to the writings of the early Church fathers (especially of the Alexandrian school), is that the Jews *en masse* and a practical totality rejected Messiah. Nevertheless, the events of Acts 2, which occur at the time of Shavuot (Pentecost), and this very account by James seem to indicate otherwise. The success of the early *ekklesia* is due to these many thousands of Jews, who believe in the Messiah and are "zealous for the Law." It is not a question that most Jewish people in Jerusalem rejected the Messiah and that the major thrust of Judaism today holds to the rejection of Jesus. However, population estimates for Jerusalem at about 70AD indicate between 80,000-400,000 people and could indicate a significant number of believers, per capita, in Jerusalem at the time of Acts 21.[6]

Luke writes that it was reported to James that Paul had been telling the Jews who were among the Gentiles not to circumcise their children and to "forsake Moses." However, the Greek actually indicates something much stronger than merely forsaking the person of Moses. In fact, Paul is being accused of apostasy (*apostasian*), which is the Greek word that is translated "forsake." This is a very serious charge indeed! Paul is being accused of no less than apostasy.

Apostasy: An Excursus

A subtle but important distinction is in order: the difference between forsaking and apostatizing. Firstly, *apostasian* means only one thing in the Greek text: to abandon the one true religion. *Kataleipo*, on the other hand means "forsaking." However, this type of forsaking

---

6   David H. Stern, *Jewish New Testament Commentary* (Jewish New Testament Publications, 1996), 301; Ariel and D'vorah Berkowitz, *Torah Rediscovered*, 5th ed. (Shoreshim Publishing, Inc., 2012), 109.

seems to be used in reference to relationships between people (Mt. 27:46; Mk. 15:34; Acts 2:27, 31; 2 Cor. 4:9; 2 Tim. 4:10; Heb. 13:5). There is however an important connection made by Peter in 2 Peter 2:15 (*kataleipo*) that connects this type of relational forsaking of the "right path" with a deeper doctrinal and divine forsaking of the the Commandment of God, which is found a few verses later in 2 Peter 2:21 (*hypostrepho*).[7] This is quite similar to Jeremiah's usage in Jeremiah 2:19, where the Septuagint translates "apostasies" from *apostasia* and "forsake" from *kataleipo*.[8] Thus, a spiritual and doctrinal "forsaking" (i.e., apostasy) is more precisely conveyed in words like *apostasian*, *hypostrepho*, *apostrepho* (Hos. 14:4 LXX), and *parapipto*.[9] These words are more indicative of orthodoxy, orthopraxy, orthopathy, and one's state of belief and how they live that belief out. In fact, the antonyms of these terms are *epistrepho* and *metanoia*, which literally mean "to turn toward"—referring to a change in mind and disposition, or in other words, repentance. The emphasis of this concept is on the recognition of wrongdoing, admission of wrongs, and then walking in a manner that is in alignment with the ways of God. Therefore, when one commits apostasy, they forsake (*kataleipo*) their relationship with the Most High and the community of believers and are liable for a certificate of divorce, a word which just so happens to share the same root as apostasy (see *apostasion*)! Of course, this notion of divorce is

---

7   Verse 15: "Forsaking (*kataleipo*) the right way, they have gone astray, having followed the way of Balaam, the son of Beor, who loved the wages of unrighteousness." Verse. 21: "For it would be better for them not to have known the way of righteousness than having known it, to turn away (*hypostrepho*) from the holy commandment handed on to them.

8   "'Your own wickedness will correct you, and your apostasies (*apostasia*) will reprove you; Know therefore and see that it is evil and bitter for you to forsake (*kataleipo*) the LORD your God, and the dread of Me is not in you,' declares the Lord GOD of hosts."

9   Heb. 6:6; Ez. 14:13; 15:8.

directly applicable to the bride of Christ; much of the covenantal language of the New Covenant is cast in marital terminology (e.g., Jer. 31:31-33 which says, "although I was a husband to them"). Apostasy, for all intents and purposes *is* adultery and could be cause for a certificate of divorce (*apostasion*).[10] Therefore, *apostasia* and *kataleipo* are not synonyms; rather, personal forsaking is what happens between people as result of apostasy (i.e., being "cut off from your people").[11] Hence, it is important that Luke used *apostasia* in Acts 21 because, if the charge of apostasy were true, then the result would have been a personal forsaking of Paul (*kataleipo*). In much the same way, the act of *apostasia* (violating and leaving the rules of the marriage covenant) leads to *apostasion* (divorce) and *kataleipo* (personal forsaking) from the Most High.

Furthermore, the word *apostasia* occurs only twice in the Apostolic writings: here in Acts 21, and in 2 Thessalonians 2:3, where it refers to the man of lawlessness and the great apostasy. Interestingly,

---

10   There is an argument that claims that Adonai divorced Israel because they broke the Covenant. This argument uses Deut. 24:1-4 in connection with texts like Jeremiah 3 and Hebews 9 in an attempt to show that God has to die and become a new man in order for him to remarry his people—that somehow in Christ's hypostatic union and via the resurrection, his historically new ontology as truly man and truly God makes him a new man and thus is allowed to marry the wayward bride. This argument is insufficient because, although Israel was unfaithful to the covenant (Jer. 31; Ex. 32), the law in the Torah about divorce is quite specific. Deut. 24:1-4 details that the original husband cannot remarry the wife only if she had married another man who had also divorced her. Since Israel did not marry another man (although she did show unfaithfulness, playing the harlot), she is never shown as marrying another. On this note, even at the height of Israel's harlotry, there was always a faithful remnant who did not bend the knee and worship other gods. Secondly, Christ's death is more indicative of atonement as opposed to a legal loop-hole that allows him to remarry his people after a divorce. In fact, Christ's death is the very sacrifice needed to overcome these intentional acts of apostasy.

11   See Mt. 18:15-20; 1 Cor. 5:5.

in 2 Thessalonians 2, *apostasia* is directly translated as "apostasy" in English Bibles, rather than "forsake" as it is in Acts 21.[12] Similarly, the translators should have rendered James's discourse in Acts 21 as "apostasy from Moses." This is a more direct and accurate description. However, that translation would clearly indicate that adherence to the Law of Moses and at least some of the "customs" were part and parcel with the one true religion, over thirty years after the resurrection! Perhaps interpretative bias is at play due to theological antinomian commitments, or maybe there is confusion between *kataleipo* and *apostasia* as synonyms? Either way, the charge of apostasy is much more significant than simply turning away from Moses as a person, which is what the word 'forsake' (and its more typical source of *kataleipo*) would indicate. Additionally, how one interprets the concept of the one true religion in Acts 21 could have significant implications for understanding 2 Thessalonians 2:3. Specifically, it raises questions such as: What Law is the man of lawlessness violating, and which doctrinal aspects of the one true faith must people reject in order to bring about the great apostasy? Based on James' and Paul's interaction in Acts 21, it seems that the Law spoken of is none other than that written by the hand of Moses, lived out and interpreted by Christ, and then lived out and taught by the apostles. Thus, leaving the commandments given by Moses is the most likely definition of apostasy, and the means by which one leaves covenant with God. The refusal of abiding in the commandments (*practicing* lawlessness) is the single greatest marker of an apostate.

---

12   Although there is a school of thought that considers the great apostasy to be the "rapture," the context of lawlessness (the man of lawlessness) and those who follow that path (the apostates) renders this view quite unlikely. Nowhere in Scripture is the word *apostasia* used in the context of current believers; it is always of those who have abandoned the faith.

The Source of the Trial: Galatians and How it Connects to Acts 21

While the majority of commentators often cite Galatians as evidence of Torah-abolition, it's quite interesting that within the Book of Galatians, Paul notes that Peter, James, and John added nothing to his gospel during his visit to Jerusalem. The historical setting of the Book of Galatians, being written about thirty years after the resurrection, places it among the earliest and most important of Paul's letters (remember that the earliest orthopraxy is the best orthopraxy). It seems reasonable that if Christ's purpose was to partially or completely abolish the Law of Moses—as supposedly taught by the apostles—this doctrine would have been clearly worked out between James, John, Peter, and Paul over the course of thirty years (Gal. 2:6), and the believers under their guidance would *not* still be zealous for the Law. But then why are there *myriads* of believers who are zealous for the Law (Acts 21:20)? Have the Jewish and Gentile believers under the apostles' instruction not understood their newfound freedom from Moses? Surely, if the apostles had indeed taught Torah-abolition, such zeal for the Law would not persist after thirty years of Apostolic instruction and after the writing of Galatians.

Furthermore, from a logical standpoint and considering the widely accepted timeline, if Paul's message of Mosaic-discontinuity had been approved by James, Peter, and John as indicated in Galatians 2, then why would James later question Paul about preaching apostasy from Moses, as seen here in Acts 21?[13] Based on the timing of Paul's travel

---

13   What has escaped most interpreters is that Gentiles were not privy to the Law of Moses and so had no knowledge of being under anything written by Moses. Instead, Gentiles were alone and without God in the world. Thus, the message of Torah abrogation would have only really been relevant to the Jews. See Harold W. Hoehner, *Ephesians: An Exegetical Commentary* (Baker Academic, 2002), 376.

to the Galatians, there would have been no question that Paul was teaching the cessation and abolition of Moses because that message would have been approved by council *before* the writing of Galatians. If Paul's Gospel had already received approval, the pressing question is why the charade of Acts 21?

To recap, historical analysis shows that the events of the second Jerusalem council (Acts 21) take place *after* the writing of the epistles to the Galatians (and likely even 1 Thessalonians and Romans), which is the very book cited by most interpreters to argue for Torah-abolition. So again, why the charade of the second Jerusalem council?[14] Perhaps a blunt answer is that the Apostles must lie to keep the peace in Jerusalem. However, if that were true, it would make them either outright liars at worst, or doctrinally contradictory at best. Perhaps, like Bultmann indicates, they are in the process of making up a new Greek religion and have yet to cast off the old vestiges of Jewish thought.[15] Thus, their theology is moving or transitory.[16] Alternatively, they are simply being "all things to all men," which is the typical interpretation within evangelical thought. The crux of this evangelical interpretation uses 1 Corinthians 9:19-23 in connection with the popular interpretation of Peter's vision in Acts 10 and 11 to explain Paul's actions in Acts 21. Thus, in Acts 21, Paul is simply being conciliatory to the Jews while actually truly teaching Mosaic abolition. Or perhaps more cynically,

---

14 A well accepted historical timeline would be (1) Peter's vision in Acts 10-11, (2) Paul's actions and writing in Galatians, 1 Thessalonians, and the writing of James's Epistle, (3) the first Jerusalem council (Acts 15) and Romans, and (4) the second Jerusalem Council (Acts 21).

15 Rudolph Bultmann, *Primitive Christianity in its Contemporary Setting* (Meridian Books, 1956).

16 Merrill C. Tenney, *New Testament Survey*, Revised by Walter M. Dunnett (Eerdmans, 1985), 246-255.

the apostles are doctrinal chameleons, considering the extreme variance in orthopraxy between Jew and Greek, of which there is supposed to be no separation (Rom. 10:12).

Surely, there is a solution to these "hard to understand" things Paul has been saying in the Diaspora (2 Pet. 3:16). The interpretations discussed above have given rise to the following options:

1. **Liars:** Paul, James, and Peter are liars and cannot be trusted.
2. **Mentally Disordered:** They are liars, but because of mental disorders. So, although they are guilty, they can be excused on medical grounds.
3. **Truth Tellers:** Paul is truthful. James, Peter, John, and Paul are practicing the one true religion and walking orderly, keeping the Law of Moses. If Paul is a truth teller, there are three interpretations:

a. **Transitory:** Paul, along with James, Peter, and John, is creating a new religion, and the vestiges of Jewish practice have yet to be cast off. Thus, they are not contradictory, but evolving, and perhaps evolving with God as Process Theology claims. The book of Acts is evidence of the growing pains spurred by the Holy Spirit.

b. **Appeasement/Conciliation/Compromise:** Paul, James, and Peter know that the Law of Moses has been partially or fully abolished but continue to walk in the Mosaic and Rabbinic traditions when they need to, whether to keep the peace, for prudential self-interest, or for the sake of the gospel. Therefore, it is not contradictory to be "all things to all men" and also maintain that there is no separation between the natural sons of Abraham (Jews) and the adopted sons (Gentiles). This is the typical view of Evangelical and Reformed Christianity.[17]

c. **Continuous:** The Law of God as written by Moses and the profitable traditions (paradosis/dogmata) are fully applicable and enforceable by the Apostles to both Jews and Gentiles.[18] This is the view defended here and is prevalent in certain strands of Messianic Judaism and Pronomian Christianity.

Either Paul or a Bad Man: In Context

As stated above, there are only two possible explanations for Paul's actions in the Diaspora: either he is preaching a message of apostasy from the Law of Moses, or he is not. James' words indicate that Paul is not preaching apostasy, saying, "all will know that there is nothing to the things which they have been told about you, but that you yourself also walk orderly, keeping the Law" (Acts 21:24). So, with relative ease, one can determine that Paul is not preaching apostasy from Moses.

---

17 John B. Polhill, *Acts*, vol. 26, The New American Commentary (Broadman and Holman, 1992), 449-450.

18 Acts 16:4; 2 Thess, 2:15. Examples abound in the gospel accounts of Christ following rabbinic *halakhot* that are not explicitly commanded by the Word of God given by the hand of Moses, which although codified later (2nd, 3rd, 4th centuries CE) have obvious connections to that of 1st century Judaisms. Mt. 9:14-15 (Cp. b. *Sukkah* 25b.; t. *Berchot* 2.10). Mt. 10:24 (b. *Berachot* 58b.; *Sifra* §251.2). Mt. 12:5 (Cp. b. *Shabbat* 132b.). Mt. 15:1 (Cf. m. *Chagigah* 2.5; b. *Shabbat* 13b-14a; y. *Shabbat* 1.3d; b. *Yoma* 87a). Mt. 15:36 (The Torah only speaks to blessing God after a meal). Mt. 22:40 (cp. m. *Chagigah* 1.8; b. *Berachot* 63a). Mt. 23:16,17 (cf. m. *Nedarim* 1.3,4; b. *Temurah* 32a-33b); Mt. 23:23 (cp. m. *Maasarot* 1.1; b. *Yoma* 83b; b. *Nidah* 5a; b. *Rosh HaShanah* 12a; b. *Shabbat* 68a.); Mt. 24:20 (cf. b. *Erubin* 4.5; Acts 1:12, Jer. 17:19-22); Mt. 26:20 (Cf. b. *Pasachim* 10:1).; Mt. 27:6 (b. *Aboda Zera* 17a); Lk. 6:9 (Cp. m. *Shabbat* 22.5); Lk. 11:44 (m. *Oholot* 16.1,2); Jn. 7:51(Mid. Rab. *Exodus* 23.1). See Tim Hegg, *Paul's Epistle to the Galatians* (Torah Resource, 2010), 18-19 for a fuller explanation of each instance.

Given these words from James, there are only three options for the interpreter of the text: (1) Paul is lying to James, (2) Paul is lying to James because Paul is insane, or (3) Paul is telling the truth and is not preaching apostasy from Moses.

Did Paul Lie to James?

Could it be possible that Paul lied to James? Surely, all men are fallible and can succumb to peer pressure like Peter did (Gal. 2). However, nowhere in the Bible do the other apostles indicate that Paul made such an error. In fact, the context of Acts 21 is the trial ensuring that Paul did *not* lie to the others. Should Paul be lying, he makes the lie so convincing as to participate in one of the most sacred ceremonies available to non-Levites and one specifically designed to show one's commitment to the Most High. If Paul did lie to James, the consequences would, of course, be dire for the status of most of the New Testament. Given that Acts 21 occurs after Paul's writings of Galatians, 1 Thessalonians, and Romans, Paul's insistence on following the Law of Moses would cast doubt on the doctrinal validity of those epistles because the central message of those epistles *seems* to advocate for antinomianism (or so the argument goes), while Paul's statements to James in Acts 21 suggest precisely the opposite. In other words, Paul preached and wrote about apostatizing from Moses (allegedly) in those early texts, but then indicated to James that he did not. In short, the Pauline corpus (at least Galatians, Thessalonians, and Romans) ought to be abandoned if Paul is a liar. Furthermore, should Paul have lied, then Peter's words would be false in 2 Peter 3:16. This option, for all intents and purposes, makes Paul a false apostle, and the books of Peter, James, and John suspect.

However, since James, John, and Peter indicate that Paul *did not* lie to them, this option is unlikely. Multiple sources—including those from Luke, who traveled with Paul, as well as from James, Peter, and John—indicate that Paul remained honest and trustworthy until the end. In fact, it was Paul who even corrected Peter's hypocrisy after the first Jerusalem council (Gal. 2). Furthermore, the very context of Acts 21 is James' fact-finding mission to determine if Paul was lying about the gospel he was preaching. Remember, Galatians records that "they added nothing to me." Therefore, one can conclude that Acts 21 is James' attempt to find out if Paul's gospel had in fact changed. Given all this and the verdict given by this impromptu trial, it seems safe to assume that Paul did not lie to James in Acts 21.

Additionally, given Paul's polemic against the "false brethren" in Galatians and that Acts 21 most certainly occurs after the writing of Galatians, it seems that neither Paul nor James would have referred to these zealous persons as *believers* if they were the "false brethren" (Acts 21:20; Gal. 2:5). Since the "false brethren" were already identified at the First Jerusalem Council and by Paul in Galatians, it is unlikely that these many thousands of *believers* here in Acts 21 were associated with either the Gentile Judaizers or the Party of the Circumcision.[19] Even

---

19 Although the term "Judaizer" has had various meanings, it is generally defined as individuals of Jewish descent or Gentiles who have undergone proselyte circumcision and who required both circumcision and full adherence to the Law of Moses for inclusion in the covenants. See Paul W. Barnett, *Jesus and the Logic of History, New Studies in Biblical Theology*, vol. 3, ed. D.A. Carson (IVP, 1997), 125-126. I use the term "Gentile Judaizers" to make a distinction between the Gentiles who accepted proselyte circumcision from the original agitators who demanded circumcision, probably Pharisaical Jews. Although this identification need not be monolithic, as it seems Paul is also addressing Gentiles who became members of the Party of the Circumcision for any number of reasons, either through their concern about the prosecution that would ensue either from Rome or from unbelieving Jews. See A.J. Goddard and S.A. Cummins, "Ill or Ill-Treated? *Conflict and Persecution as the Context of Paul's Original Ministry in Galatia* (Galatians 4:12-20)," Journal for the Study of the New Testament 52 (1993), 93-126.; Richard N. Longenecker,

with their zeal for the Torah and their adherence to the customs, it is quite unlikely that Paul and James would give heed to their charges if they were considered to be "false brethren." If Paul had performed a sacred ceremony to appease the "false brethren," it would have lent credence to their doctrines and made Paul a doctrinal liar.[20] Rather, it seems that these *believers* are, for all intents and purposes, accepted by James and Paul as legitimate and aligned with their teaching. This raises the question: why the uproar? The believers had heard something that went against what they thought to be true. So, was Paul lying to them? If not, what is the explanation? James provides the answer: Paul walked orderly, keeping the Law. But before we settle on that answer, we must briefly comment on the second option.

Is Paul a Madman?

So, Paul did not lie to James. However, one possibility that seems overlooked is that Paul might have been insane. Perhaps much of the confusion about Paul stems from the fact that his mental faculties were in such disorder that he could in fact say two mutually exclusive things (apostasy from Moses and upholding the Law of Moses) and think that he was in his right mind. The notion that Paul had a

---

Galatians, Word Biblical Commentary 41, ed. Bruce M. Metzger (Word, 1990), 291. Dunn, likewise, underscores how when those Gentiles in Galatia undertook proselyte circumcision for salvation they were putting themselves under the whole bondage of Pharisaical oral law as Judaizing Gentiles. D.G. Dunn, *The Epistle to the Galatians*, Black's New Testament Commentary, ed. Henry Chadwick (Eerdmans, 1996), 226. Hegg also underscores that Judaizing is more indicative of Gentile acceptance of circumcision as the foundation of covenant inclusion and the starting point of grace. See Tim Hegg, *The Letter Writer*, 106. What I wish to show is that "Judaizing" is more indicative of the motive for circumcision, and that Torah observance as obedience is not necessarily part of that definition.

20   Acts 15:1; 2 Cor. 11:13, 26; Gal. 2:4; Phil. 3:2; 2 Thess. 2:11.

mental disorder could also explain his conversion experience and his claim to be an apostle of Christ. Maybe Paul merely imagined Christ's appearance to him, and his blindness on the road to Damascus was the result of a psychotic episode, which in turn led him to deceive the apostles in Jerusalem. It so happens that medically unexplained vision loss, or non-organic visual loss (NOVL), is a well-established condition believed to be caused by psychological factors.[21] Perhaps Paul's reclusion to Arabia was merely the result of delusions of grandeur or mental decay caused by *pharmakeia* or possible schizophrenia. This could also explain Paul's vocabulary using words like "my gospel" and his insistence of being the apostle to the Gentiles—he simply *thought* that he was a religious leader and the founder of the new allegorical Greek religion (e.g., Bultmann and the transitory theory, but caused by insanity). When confronted by James in Acts 21 about his alleged apostasy, Paul could genuinely maintain both positions. He did not preach apostasy; rather, his message and gospel incorporated both the abolition and the upholding of the Law as doctrine. In a sense, Paul is lying to James but only because of mental disorder and the doctrinal disarray caused by his illness. His contradictory/transitory doctrines would have been similar to that of Eastern pantheistic religions, where the disciples have to chase the thoughts of the shaman, like birds fluttering in the wind, affirming opposites (good/evil and sin/righteousness) as one. As the founder of a new religion, however, and the only one given the special revelation (i.e., something akin to Joseph Smith), he alone held the secrets to how this mystery of the gospel could be

---

21 Raj Persaud, M.D. and Peter Bruggen, M.D., "Can you Lose Your Eyesight for Psychological Reasons," *Psychology Today*, https://www.psychologytoday.com/us/blog/slightly-blighty/201508/can-you-lose-your-eyesight-psychological-reasons (Aug 17, 2015).

solved, the simultaneous obedience and apostasy from Moses being Paul's own deluded creation.

If Paul had a mental illness that was the cause of his doctrinal confusion (whether it be the contradictory, transitory, or even the conciliatory theories), one could in fact forgive Paul. He did not choose his mental illness, but as a result, we should not rely on him for doctrine. His writings should be viewed in a similar light to Nietzsche's later works—simply the ramblings of a psychotic Jewish rabbi.

Therein lies the rub. Paul's writings do not appear to be the work of a madman. In fact, they are far from it. For example, the use of irony in the book of Galatians indicates a sound and robust mind.[22] Furthermore, Romans stands out as one of the finer pieces of doctrinal and philosophical thought in the entire canon. It offers a profound exploration of the Abrahamic Covenant, the Mosaic Covenant, the New Covenant, the inclusion of Gentiles in these covenants, and Christ's work for both Jews and Greeks. In contrast to Nietzsche's final writings, which reflect the thoughts of a veritable madman, Paul's cogency and coherence (his doctrinal consistency) is surely the mark of a sane, sober, moral, and prudent person. Trained under Gamaliel and, most importantly, trusted by Luke, James, Peter, and John, Paul's writings reflect the work of a sound mind.

Paul the Truth Teller

The conclusion we must draw, then, is that since Paul is neither a liar nor a madman, the most logical and well-supported option is that Paul is indeed telling the truth! This means that he is not preaching or writing about apostasy from Moses, but instead, as James said, he walks orderly, keeping the Law. To concretely demonstrate Paul's doc-

---

22   Mark Nanos, *The Irony of Galatians* (Fortress, 2002), 127.

trinal orthodoxy to all present in Jerusalem, Paul is directed by James to perform sacrificial and ceremonial laws, which are, in all likelihood, the Nazirite Vow of Numbers 6. This is meant to show this orderliness and his perseverance in the gospel approved by James, Peter, and John (cf. Rev. 14:12).

Sacrifices after the Resurrection: The Theological Conundrum

One of the most paradigmatic confirming evidences comes from the fact that, even after over thirty years, James was overseeing men who were sacrificing at the Temple and ordered Paul to do the same *to confirm* his gospel message and to show that he walked orderly, keeping the Law.[23] Given that more than thirty years had passed since the resurrection, if the sacrificial system was no longer part of the apostles' and early believers' doctrine, that teaching would have been both practiced and preached. However, what we see here is quite the opposite. Therefore, from a historical perspective, the very *earliest* doctrine of the apostles in Jerusalem was faith in the Messiah and orderly walking, according to the requirements of the Torah, including the ceremonial components.[24] If those commandments were no longer required or had been abrogated in some way through Christ, the message of abrogation would have been proclaimed and *applied equally to both Jew and Gentile*: "Christ freed us from the bondage of

---

23   One even sees that Peter and others were in the Temple continuously praising God (Lk. 24:53).

24   Richard Bauckham makes the case that "the earliest Christology is the best Christology." Surely this axiom could be applied here. If the earliest orthodoxy includes following the commandments of Moses, then perhaps it is the best orthodoxy! Richard Bauckham, *Jesus and the God of Israel: God Crucified and other Studies on the New Testament's Christology of Divine Identity* (Eerdmans, 2008), 128-130, 195-210.

Moses! Go tell it on the mountain! We are free!" However, this does not correspond with the information presented in Acts 21. In short, what the impromptu trial gave the apostles was the golden opportunity to cement forever the understanding of Mosaic discontinuity, *especially the sacrificial requirements*, but they did not. Rather, James insists that Paul perform Mosaic sacrifices, even in light of the Messiah, to show *doctrinal purity*. Although a plain reading of Acts 21 and its context suggests Mosaic continuity as a straightforward conclusion, various theological theories have emerged to support an antinomian view and explain why Paul, James, Peter, and John would continue observing Mosaic practices after the resurrection and after Paul's message to the Galatians. The key question becomes: is the Apostles' interpretation of Christ and Moses transitory, conciliatory, or continuous? That is the question we will explore in the following chapters.

CHAPTER 2
TRANSITION AND EVOLUTION

The transitory interpretation of Acts 21 rests on the assumption that Paul was telling the truth in Acts 21 (i.e., walking orderly, keeping the Law), but that he was in the process of gradually developing a new religion because of Christ.[1] Thus, doctrinal "truth" was *changing* during this period, and the book of Acts reflects the growing pains between the believers in Jerusalem, who maintained Law-observance, and the emerging Law-free faith of the Gentiles. Transitory theology believes that in some form or fashion, there is an evolution in religious and doctrinal understanding showing why the apostles perform now "unnecessary" Mosaic requirements. This accounts for why the apostles required Paul to fulfill a Nazirite vow (Acts 21:21), instructed Gentiles to learn the Law of Moses every Sabbath (Acts 15:21), took part in Temple services (Acts 2), and prescribed circumcision for Timothy but not for Titus (Acts 16). The apostles eventually came to realize that the Laws of Moses were not actually required, which explains why the modern church does not follow the same practices seen in the Book of Acts.[2] Paul, being the foremost and most evolved of his apostolic contemporaries, is of course the most antinomian, as both the Johannine epistles and James's epistle still cling to Moses as central in under-

---

1   Oscar Cullmann, *The Earliest Christian Confessions*, trans. J.K.S. Reid, eds. Gary Habermas and Benjamin Charles Shaw (Wipf and Stock, 2018), 28.

2   Inherent in this position is that there is no difficultly in that Moses and the apostles (and all the prophets in between) could write contradictory things. Evolution is not contradiction, so the whole Bible is in fact a transitory and evolutionary, and all the writers are writing "truth" from their perspective. In short, the transitory theory is the preferred theory of "liberal" and post-modern theology.

standing.[3] This position posits that the *transition* to Greek Christianity was in some form a revolutionary understanding with Paul who stood in tension with the earliest Jewish believers in Jerusalem. This tension persisted, and true doctrine may not have been fully settled until much later—possibly not until centuries afterward, with the formalization of theological beliefs in the creedal statements and declarations of the councils.[4] Consequently, the real thrust of the transitory theory is best described as an intellectual attempt to reconcile seemingly contradictory doctrine and practice along an evolutionary, existential, and ecclesiastical timeline. It explains how Paul could both follow the Mosaic Law while also abrogating it or developing a new religion(s). Most significantly, it sheds light on why the Church today does not imitate the early behaviors of the apostles.[5]

At first glance, it could be easy to accept this view, based on a very common Christian experience, which is why the transitory theory has a bit of attractiveness and *prima facie* correspondence to the real

---

3   Daniel Marguerat, *Paul in Acts and Paul in His Letters* (Tübingen, Germany: Mohr Siebeck, 2013), 46-47.; Karl L. Oakes, *From Torah to Paul: The Prehistory of the Catholic Church* (Wipf and Stock, 2016), 87-97.

4   Bultmann is the foremost popular proponent of this theory, but the supersessionist ideas stretch back much farther. Bultmann's theological inventions include the development of the Christ character superimposed onto existing Greek mythology and that the earliest Church was in the process of Christianizing pagan belief and platonic philosophy. See Bultmann, *Primitive Christianity in its Contemporary Setting* (Meridian Books, 1956). There is a significant amount of theological and philosophical assumptions (dualism / existentialism) that is informing this position, which is unfortunately outside the scope of this book.

5   Considering the proliferation of Christian denominations and traditions that have sprouted, the transitory theory seems to fall along the lines of Lindbeck's ecumenical post-Liberal approach. In that, as the transition(s) occurred, the obvious result would be divisions which need synthesizing. See George A. Lindbeck, *The Nature of Doctrine: Religion and Theology in a Postliberal Age* (Westminster John Knox Press, 2009).

world. This experience is that of growing in understanding of truth. Is not sanctification the process of growing in wisdom, knowledge, and righteousness? Are not the multiplicity of denominations the results of this process? This position is given further credence when one considers that the apostles were eyewitnesses to the life of the Messiah and what he taught, and they still struggled at times to understand his teachings and needed further explanation after the resurrection. So, in this regard, the transitory theory already carries a bit of strength. Of course, growing in understanding of *preexisting* truth or *reorienting* back toward truth is not quite the same thing as truth evolving and doctrine being transitory and fluid. (This is not to say that the reorientation cannot not be radical as to have the appearance of climatic fulfillment.) Therefore, whatever weight the transitory theory carries is tainted by its inherent moral, doctrinal, and theological subjectivity. So, despite the similarity to "transitioning" belief in an individual experience, the transitory interpretation inherently assumes a bibliology that is evolutionary, doctrinally relative, and based purely in human existentialism.

The transitory theory is typically inspired by theological naturalism and is rooted in the naturalistic existential demythologization of hermeneutics, as developed by thinkers like Bultmann, Heidegger, Schleiermacher, and others. In essence, what these theologians proposed was that everything said about God in the Bible came from pre-scientific and primitive peoples.[6] Today's people are much more sophisticated and have a "scientific worldview," and, since the time of Kant and Newton, one can no longer scientifically think that God actually

---

6   Obviously, the narratives of God either creating or intervening in the world are false in light of evolutionary "facts" (paradigmatic lenses). In fact, some like Barbara King even claim that our religious tendencies toward beneficence and spirituality are directly from our supposed primate ancestors. Barbara J. King, *Evolving God: A Provocative View on the Origins of Religion* (University of Chicago Press, 2017).

enters the world to interact with his creatures. All that is myth and rather sentimental.[7] Rather, true faith today has transitioned to a more authentic and naturalistic existentialism, as God is closed off from direct interaction in a form of deistic naturalism. In essence, by ridding hermeneutics of myth, the transcendental God, who is radically, wholly other, could meet and transform people now through the Church's kerygma of God that acts upon an individual, thus transforming them.[8] The Bible, however, as evidenced by its contradictions (primarily here in Acts 21) and prescientific mythology, is rendered a purely human construct, devoid of the actual word of God, and it only *becomes* the kerygmatic word of God in the individual.[9] This internal revelation thus leads to new "authentic" moral and spiritual transformation. In short, this version of the transitory theory is based on cosmological, epistemological, and existential assumptions that lead to naturalistic, autonomistic, experiential theology. Through this reasoning, one can see how Paul and James could have various understandings and that they could contradict one another but still be true because they were being *authentic* to the "Word" they interpreted initially. Pauline theology is simply his self-understanding, as the apostle to the Gentiles, in the same fashion that James's theology is his understanding derived from his cultural context in Jerusalem. The transitory theory therefore posits that the changing doctrine found primarily in Paul is the authen-

---

7   C.S. Lewis, *Voyage of the Dawn Treader* (Harper, 1994), 16.

8   John Morrison, *Has God Said?*, Loc. 1164 (Kindle).

9   Karl Barth, *Church Dogmatics* I/1. trans. G. Thompson (T&T Clark, 1936), 123-124. Although I believe Barth would reject the Panentheistic views of Process theology, Barth's Bibliology and emphasis on authenticity and the written word becoming the true word of God in us by the Spirit is indicative of transitional theologians and is probably strongly influenced by his Reformed Supersessionism and the allegorical hermeneutics of Augustine.

tic self-discovery of doctrine developed over time by the apostles, and the Book of Acts is the supposed self-discovery *process* by the collective. As in, the transitory position views the modern expression of the church, beginning with the apostles, as the development from mustard seed to full grown tree. Therefore, the doctrine should not be viewed as contradictory, but as evolutionary, and correctly revolutionary by its casting off the chains of Mosaic tyranny.

The scientific and dualist theological methods of transitory theology also birthed the idea of the evolving God of Process Theology.[10] Scripture had to evolve because "God" was evolving and interacting with his creation in more advanced ways to persuade his creation. Since "God" was evolving and expressing this evolution, and since humans were also evolving in their own thoughts about "God," these interactions of divine and human freewill were then written down, and those

---

10   Process Theology is the result of the Process philosophical paradigm that was championed by Alfred Whitehead and then turned into theology by Charles Hartshorne and John Cobb. As the case may be, this theo-philosophical paradigm necessitates that God changes as the self-deterministic creatures interact with one another. "God" cannot coerce anything to happen; rather, "God" attempts to influence desired outcomes according to "his" values. Furthermore, this theology proclaims that "God" contains the universe, but is not necessarily identical with it (panentheism). Although the world and "God's" methods of persuasion may change, this theo-philosophical worldview claims objective morality is found only in "God," and even though "God" changes, the moral rules somehow remain the same, which I believe exposes this theology to the venom of Euthyphro's dilemma, which will be examined in the next chapter. Like many of the materialistic paradigms, the process theologians have issues with an omnipotent God allowing evil, and they also view the creation narrative in Genesis as false in light of evolutionary theory. See Alfred Whitehead, *Process and Reality: An Essay in Cosmology*, eds. David Ray Griffin and Donald W. Sherburne, (The Free Press, 1978).; Charles Hartshorne, *Divine Relativity* (Yale University Press, 1982).; John B. Cobb and David Ray Griffin, *Process Theology: An Introductory Exposition* (Westminster John Knox Press, 1976).

new writings became the scripture of the New Testament. Thus, what appears to be contradiction is not actually a contradiction but rather a process of growth, maturity, and human refinement in understanding God and his ways. It reflects the evolution of this understanding through interaction with and adaptation of his revelation to men. In these transitory theories of theology, human understanding of "God" was always in transition because "God" was transitioning in methodology of human persuasion, beginning with the mysterious Canaanite storm god El, numinous as he was, who then became the dominate God of the biblical narrative and the victor over the other gods of the ancient Near East.[11] El transitions to a more covenantal God, El Shaddai and El Elyon (The God of Abraham, Isaac, and Jacob), to transition again into Adonai, the God of Moses and the Prophets, who is morphed into a more refined Greco-Roman pagan construct, taking the form of Jesus Christ by the time of the first century. The changes in doctrine stem from "God" changing, due to the interaction with his creation and his creation interacting with him.

I would like to pose the real epistemological question: how might "God" transition in the future, and how would we recognize it? Perhaps the hypermodern usage of the prefix *trans-* is already pointing the way to the future evolving "God."[12] In any case, the transitory theory seems to accept the basic tenants of Marcionism in which Christ vanquishes the God of the Old Testament through self-evolution. Therefore, the Transitory Theory must, in a very real sense, accept Marcionism as a foundational aspect of its theology—that is, the belief that the Yahwist

---

11   O. Palmer Robertson, *The Flow of the Psalms: Discovering Their Structure and Theology* (Presbyterian and Reformed Publishing, 2015), 7740-7754 (Kindle). John N. Oswalt, *The Bible Among the Myths* (Zondervan, 2009).

12   LGBTQ Theology. See Mark A. Yarhouse, *Understanding Gender Dysphoria: Navigating Transgender Issues in a Changing Culture* (Intervarsity Press, 2015).

religion is founded upon a God who is evil and defective in some way, that Christ is the son of the true God, and that the God of the Jews is distinct from the God revealed in Jesus Christ.

Paradigms Driving Transitory Theology

To recap, one finds that the two primary theological constructs that give credence to the transitory theory are necessarily founded upon theological, cosmological, and epistemological paradigms that have serious flaws. In the demythologization of Bultmann, one finds naturalistic and deistic presuppositions that mandate the use of experiential, allegorical, and dialectical theological methods, making much of its doctrine and truth claims inherently subjective. This is due to their *a priori* rejection that God physically interacts with the world and the belief that the Bible, as it stands, is not the word of God but rather words about God, who is wholly other and utterly incomprehensible.[13] On the other hand, Process Theology rejects the naturalistic deism of Bultmann in favor of a growing and learning "God," who is changeable based on the understanding and freewill actions of the creation. This is the way Process Theology explains their version of dispensations and radically different modes of interaction between God and man, moving from the numinous and violent "God" of the Old Testament to the loving, gracious, and tolerant "God" of the New Testament.[14] Furthermore, this transition to the good God of the New Testament affirms Marcionism as truth. As "God" learned more about his free creatures he transitioned his doctrine to accommodate them

---

13   Karl Barth, *Church Dogmatics* I/2. Eds. G.W. Bromiley and T.F. Torrance (T&T Clark, 1970), 29.

14   Erich Zenger, *A God of Vengeance?: Understanding the Psalms of Divine Wrath*, trans. Linda M. Maloney (Westminster John Knox Press, 1994).

and persuade them toward divinity. Although this book is not necessarily concerned with showing these paradigms as false, what should be readily apparent is that they have significant issues in developing cohesive, comprehensive, consistent, and comely explanations of the data, primarily in the fact that God speaks and does, that he can enter into the world, and most of all, that miracles are possible.[15] Thus, the foundational *a priori* of transitory theology is severely lacking and way outside of orthodoxy, being rooted in either panentheism or naturalism. The transitory theory could, therefore, be rejected *a priori,* merely on philosophical grounds.

Hermeneutical Weakness of the Transitory Theory: No Transition Indicated in Early Historical Biblical Data

Aside from the faults of naturalistic and evolutionary *a priori* of the transitory theory, there appear to be actual hermeneutical and historical faults as well. If serious historical analysis and early testimony are the keys to understanding the faith, then the transitory theory would have started with the earliest believers and eyewitnesses of Christ's teachings, not later with Paul, and most certainly before the replacement theologies of the Church fathers.[16] Evidence that is earlier and has multiple attestation is considered the gold standard when examining facts about the past. Therefore, if it can be shown that no transition took place before Paul, it is unlikely that a transition actually occurred at all. Considering what we know already about

---

15 Craig S. Keener, *Miracles: The Credibility of the New Testament Accounts* (Baker Academic, 2012).

16 It is no surprise here as the Transitory theologians reject the historicity of many of the NT texts, thus these facts are ruled out *a priori*. According to many of the transitory theologians, they assume the writing of many NT texts come much later and suffer from significant historical reliability issues.

the trial of Paul in Acts 21, is there evidence of transition before the Pauline epistles? In short, the later the supposed transition occurs, the less historically grounded the epistemic foundations of the transition become. Even though a transition could have occurred, early sources with multiple attestations provide a window into the earliest thought and practice. If one can see what the earliest witnesses to Christ's life believed, said, and most importantly did, one can decipher the best orthodoxy and orthopraxy, and discern whether or not a transition occurred with *them*. If a transition did not occur with the earliest believers, then the transition was merely a theological creation of later generations.

No Transition on The Road to Emmaus: Early and Eyewitness Testimony in Luke 24

Firstly, Cleopas (Lk. 24:18) and Simon (Lk. 24:34) received Christ's instructions and explanation of the Law and the Prophets on the road to Emmaus (Lk. 24:27) and then told of the experience and teaching to other eleven (Lk. 24:33). In this case, Christ simply explained (Lk. 24:32) how the Law and Prophets pointed to him and his resurrection. Therefore, instead of teaching abolition, Christ was showing that the words of Moses and the Prophets were always Christ-ocentric and that the Promise of all the covenants had come.[17] Here, it becomes clear that fulfillment of the Law is not synonymous with abrogation of it. For, if one simply takes Christ at his word, as a basic truth and a hermeneutical starting point, Christ in Matthew 5:17-20

---

17 Eph. 2:12. This text is often interpreted "covenants of promise" but the Greek *diathekon* (Covenants) is plural and *epangelias* (promise) is singular. I think that a better interpretation would be "Covenants of The Promise," meaning all the covenants point to a singular promise, that being Christ.

confirms non-abolition.[18] Christ explained to Simon and Cleopas that he himself was always in the Tanakh, and that the contents therein point to him.[19] Far from being viewed in terms of abolition, the discourse is more indicative of Christ showing how to use the Torah as apologetic evidence, which ensures the Tanakh's ever-increasing importance. In essence, Christ is demonstrating through the scriptures of the Tanakh that the Messiah of Israel has come. This likewise confirms that the Tanakh is the Word of God, for its promises (particularly those to Abraham) have come to pass, and the prophesies yet fulfilled will come to pass. With all this in mind, if Christ did teach Mosaic abolition, or a transition away from Moses on the road to Emmaus, then surely the apostles would have been informed right from the very beginning, and that message would have been preached. This fact alone would thus negate even the possibility of Acts 15 or Acts 21 from happening, for the transition *would have already taken place*, and there would be no question as to the continuity of Moses. But, as the case may be, the Tanakh must be used for apologetic reasons, showing the truth of Messiah, not to mention for correction, reproof, and training in righteousness (cf. 2 Tim. 3:15-17), thus necessitating its continuity.

No Transition in the Great Commission

Secondly, the well-known "Great Commission" in Matthew 28:19-20 records an interesting requirement. It is common to quote

---

18 David Stern highlights that the term "fulfill" in reference to the Torah is a first-century idiom, which refers to proper interpretation rather than cancellation. The idiom suggests that Christ came to fully teach the Torah, revealing its intended meaning through his teachings. Rubin, *The Complete Jewish Study Bible*, 1390-1391.

19 This seems to give credibility to the interpretation of Rom. 10:4 in that Christ was the goal of the Torah.

the first part of the commission: "Go therefore and make disciples of all the nations, baptizing them in the name of the Father and the Son and the Holy Spirit…" But it's the second part of the commission that does not receive much attention. It says, "…teaching them to observe all that I commanded you; and lo, I am with you always, even to the end of the age." Now what is interesting about this is that Christ is commanding that all the nations observe *his* commands and what he commanded the apostles. I suggest that by "his commands," he must surely mean God's commands, since he is Adonai in the flesh, and he and the Father are one. Otherwise, one denies his divinity, falling into Docetism, Arianism, or the Ebionite missteps.

The real question is this: what are these commands, and how did the disciples and apostles know? Matthew 5:17-20 seems clear on the matter. Is it sensible for Christ to say that he did not come to abolish the Law or the Prophets, but that he came to abolish them by fulfilling them? That is nonsense and the epitome of a violation of the Law of Contradiction (A=-A). It seems that Christ preempts the confusion that his life, death, and resurrection might cause. Christ literally gives the command and a warning, "Do not think that I have come to abolish the Law or the Prophets…Whoever then annuls one of the least of these commandments, and teaches others to do the same, shall be called least in the kingdom of heaven…"[20] That being said, there is

---

20   Mt. 5:17-19. There is much debate as to whether or not Matthew 5:18 is equating "all being accomplished" to the death and resurrection, a notion which fundamentally hangs on Christ's words, "it is finished" in John 19:30. However, the fact that heaven and earth still exist is clear enough to assume that all "being accomplished" must refer to an eschatological state, as opposed to Christ's death and resurrection. Not to mention that the author of Hebrews says in 2:8, "But now we do not yet see all things subjected to him." Therefore, all has not been accomplished. See David Wilber, *How Jesus Fulfilled the Law: A Pronomian Pocket Guide to Matthew 5:17-20* (Pronomian Publishing, 2024), 51-74.

an even better example, where Christ seemingly demands the following of Moses. In Matthew 23, Christ gives a command, while exposing the hypocrisy of the Pharisees. Christ says, "The scribes and Pharisees have seated themselves in the chair of Moses; *therefore all that they tell you, do and observe,* but do not do according to their deeds; for they say things and do not do them" (Mt. 23:2-3, emphasis added). It seems that Christ commands the following of Moses *and* the profitable laws and customs (halacha) of the scribes and Pharisees.[21] Now, since one of Christ's commands was to hear and obey Moses in Matthew 23, and the Great Commission requires following Christ's commands, then the conclusion of believing in the risen Messiah and following his commandments would necessitate listening to and conforming oneself to the Law of Moses, as lived out and interpreted by Christ himself and as taught by the apostles.[22] This is the potential implication of the command found in the Great Commission.[23]

No Transition in the Book of James (Ya'acob)

There is some debate as to which epistle was actually the first to be written. There are three choices: 1 Thessalonians, Galatians, or James. Many biblical scholars think that James penned the very first epistle, given that he was converted before Paul (1 Cor. 15:7), and that Paul

---

21 Obvious exceptions include those traditions which replace and nullify the Law of God. If, at any time, a tradition of man makes an unbearable yoke or supplants the focus of Messiah, it is an idol and ought to be disregarded. See Mark 7:7-8; Matthew 5:20. Noel S Rabbinowitz, "Matthew 23:2-4: Does Jesus Recognize the Authority of the Pharisees and Does He Endorse Their Halakah?" *Journal of the Evangelical Theological Society* 46.3 (2003), 444-447.

22 Rabbinowitz, "Matthew 23:2-4," 446: "...Matthew presents 'Christian Judaism' as the only legitimate form of Judaism."

23 Rom. 3:31; 8:7; 1 Jn. 2:3; Heb. 10:28; Rev. 14:12.

spent at least three years in Arabia and Damascus before meeting Peter and James (Gal. 1:17-19).[24] It was during this time, and before the first Jerusalem council, that James became the leader of the sect of The Way in Jerusalem. Considering the timeline and James's confirmation of Paul's ministry in Galatians, it is likely that James's epistle was written shortly before Paul's first letter (whether Galatians or 1 Thessalonians).[25] Therefore, the Book of James and its overt pro-Law message demonstrates that one of the earliest epistles neither commands nor anticipates a transition away from Moses.[26] Furthermore, as the leader in Jerusalem, it is James himself who confronts Paul in Acts 21, trying to find out if he has committed apostasy from Moses in his teaching and whether Paul had strayed from the gospel message that had been approved.

No Transition in the Jerusalem Councils: Acts 15 and Acts 21

Although the primary focus of this book is Acts 21, a full understanding of this chapter and whether there is a transition away from Moses can only be achieved by also analyzing Acts 15. Here was the conclusion of the council in Acts 15:

> Therefore it is my judgment that we do not trouble those
> who are turning to God from among the Gentiles, but that
> we write to them that they abstain from things contaminated
> by idols and from fornication and from what is strangled and

---

24 Craig L. Blomberg, *The Historical Reliability of the New Testament: Countering the Challenges to Evangelical Christian Beliefs* (B&H, 2016), 464.

25 Ibid.

26 The "perfect Law of Liberty" is a very strong allusion pointing to the two most profound Torah Psalms (Ps. 19:7; 40:6-7; 119:45). See also *Aristeas* 31 and 1 QS 10:6, 8, 11, which describe the Torah as perfect and giving freedom.

from blood. For Moses from ancient generations has in every
city those who preach him, since he is read in the synagogues
every Sabbath.
—Acts 15:19-21

If the Law of Moses was being phased out, why would the apostles
have Gentile converts hear the Law every Sabbath? James and Paul
ought to have sheltered the Gentiles from the Law rather than exposing them to it, particularly if it was passing away while Paul was estab-
lishing a new religion for the Gentiles, as the transitory theory posits.

That, however, raises the question: *do Acts 15 or Acts 21 mandate
a transition away from Mosaic orthopraxy for believers in the Messiah?*
To answer that, it is important to establish a proper historical understanding of these chapters, considering the complex dynamics between
first-century Judaisms and their views on salvation, how Gentile believers were accepted into the community after leaving their pagan backgrounds, and why the apostles emphasized faith over circumcision in
their teachings. If neither Acts 15 nor Acts 21 show a transition, then
the transitory theory becomes seriously imperiled.

Acts 21 and Acts 15: The Core Issue of Circumcision,
First Century Soteriology, Jewish Ethnicity, and
the World To Come

Referring back to the Great Commission, one should recall that
the very emphasis of Christ is that all the believing ones from among
the nations undergo a mikveh (baptism) for the identifying marker of
association. This stands in contrast to prevalent theological thought in
Judaism at the time of Christ. In first-century Judaism, according to
oral law, proselytes were required to make a sacrifice, be circumcised,
and be immersed in a mikveh. After the destruction of the temple,

it is recorded that money equivalent to the sacrifice was required for conversion to Judaism.[27] By doing these actions, the gentile by birth could become ethnically Jewish by religious ceremony. For many in the first century, in order to be assured participation in the world to come, one not only had to practice Judaism, but one also needed to be Jewish, for only the Jews were graciously granted salvation and the covenant promises. It was the act of becoming Jewish, by circumcision, that marked entrance into the covenants, and thus granted salvation to the Gentile.[28] What Christ and the apostles underscore is that salvation is based first on faith, and that the baptism was the outward expression of that faith. Again, the primary disagreement of the time is how one enters into the covenant. This relative ease of Gentile inclusion demonstrated by Christ and the Apostles is not totally unprecedented, however, as Hillel also bucked the anti-Gentile trends in first-century Judaism. On the whole, the position of Christ marks a significant departure from rabbinic tradition, which required not only a mikveh, but also physical circumcision and sacrifices.[29]

The Sin Nature and Soteriology of the 1st Century: An Excursus

In order to understand the historical context, a brief understanding of the human condition is required. The doctrine of original sin, or, more aptly, a pervasively depraved human nature, inherited through Adam, is seemingly already understood and accepted by rabbinic authorities. In the first century, there were rabbis and sages who

---

27   b. *Yevamot* 47a; M. *Sanhedrin* 10:1.; b. *Sanhedrin* 90a.; b. *B'rachot* 5a.; 4Q521.

28   James H. Charlesworth, ed., *The Old Testament Pseudepigrapha*, Vol. 2 (Doubleday & Company, Inc., 1985), 792. See *Epic of Theodotus*.

29   Tim Hegg, *Paul the Letter Writer*, 86. See Hillel in b. *Shabbat* 17b.; b. *Shabbat* 31a.

tended to agree with Paul on the human sin nature (e.g., no one can keep the Law perfectly because humans are born with the propensity for sinning and ultimately *will* sin).[30] Therefore, it seems that it was already understood that salvation was granted by grace. The actual disagreement at hand was the *starting point* of that grace and how it was granted to the individual. The Apostles consider faith to be the initiator of grace to the individual, while the Party of the Circumcision believe that circumcision was the starting point of grace. The belief among the latter was that since Israel chose to accept the Torah, God chose the people of Israel for salvation, and as a result, anyone born into Israel was *automatically* granted a place in the world to come.[31] This grace, of course, was confirmed on the eighth day of one's life via circumcision. One could, theoretically, be cut off from the people (lose salvation), however, it was generally believed that those chosen into the Jewish community would be saved purely because of their *ethnic heritage*.[32]

Therefore, since it was already widely accepted in first-century Judaism that grace had been granted to the Jewish people, the Sages also had to consider whether, and how, Gentiles could partake in the covenant promises. According to Montegiore and Loewe, the heathen Gentiles are called enemies of God, given their entrenchment in idolatry and all manners of wickedness and are cut off from the covenants of God and without hope in the world.[33] The Rabbis' *theological* con-

---

30   *Sanhedrin* 101a. "Indeed, there is not a righteous man on earth who continually does good and who never sins." (Ecc. 7:20; Rom. 3:10-11).

31   Tim Hegg, *The Letter Writer*, 91. See *Mekilta de-Rabbi Ishmael* Exodus 20; *Midrash Rabbah* Exodus 20; b. *Avodah Zarah* 2b.

32   b. *Sanhedrin* 90a.; Thomas D. Lancaster, *The Holy Epistle to the Galatians* (FFOZ, 2011), 18-19; Shaye J.D. Cohen, "Crossing the Boundary and Becoming a Jew," *Harvard Theological Review* 82.1(1989), 27.

33   C.G. Montegiore and H.M.J Loewe, eds., *A Rabbinic Anthology* (Cambridge University

clusion was that for Gentiles to attain righteous standing before God, they would need to undergo circumcision according to the Law and become Jewish, as Jewish status was considered the basis for salvation.[34] Circumcision would mark entry into the covenant, and this newly acquired Jewish proselyte status would be maintained through continued observance of the commandments.[35]

The Transitory Theory, Gentile Inclusion, and the Reason for Acts 15

The transitory theory and the conciliatory theory both posit a change from the Law to grace. However, the fact that even the Jews of the first century understood salvation by grace (albeit incorrectly tying it to ethnicity) demonstrates that the biblical truth of grace did not emerge after the resurrection. As evidenced above, grace was already understood, even though it was misapplied.[36] Therefore, Christ's

---

Press, 2012), 556-579.; Eph. 2:12. Here it seems that Paul actually does agree with a portion of the Party of the Circumcision's argument—that is, that the Gentiles were indeed excluded from Israel and the promises of the covenants, and thus without hope.

34 b. *Yevamot* 47a.

35 Obtaining the Jewish righteous status, however, does not necessarily mean that there was not disagreements about actual societal status after Gentile conversion, with some Rabbis giving full status to Gentiles and others treating the Gentile proselytes as hardly better than slaves. In many cases it seems that, unlike modern religion, an outsider could not simply convert to Judaism and that genealogical impurity was irreparable in the Gentiles. Matthew Thiessen, *Contesting Conversion* (Oxford University Press, 2011), 148.; C.G. Montegiore and H.M.J Loewe, eds., A Rabbinic Anthology), 570.; m. *Horayot* 3:8; m. *Bikkurim* 1:4.

36 M. *Sanhedrin* 10:1.; b. *Sanhedrin* 90a.; b. *B'rachot* 5a.; 4Q521. It should also be noted here, too, that much of the Pharisaical and Essene literature contains strong references to the resurrection of the body, but only those who were Jews or proselytes would be resurrected. If the Mishna is at least partially indicative of prevailing thought in the first century, it shows that the sages already understood that perfect obedience to the Torah

instructions for the Gentiles to undergo a ritual bath symbolizing their faith and the forgiveness of their sins, as opposed to a shift away from the Law, as the transitory theory claims. In other words, Christ and Paul are correcting faulty theological conclusions about soteriology within Judaism, not radically changing the concept of grace. The Jewish sect of "The Way," contra the primary Jewish belief in the first century or the practice of certain Gentiles undergoing circumcision through the proselyte ceremony, determined that faith is the true entry point into the covenants. Grace is received and affirmed through faith, baptism, and abiding in the commands of God.

To that end, the opening verses of Acts 15 clearly illustrate why the Jerusalem council was needed:

> Some men came down from Judea and *began* teaching the brethren, "**Unless you are circumcised according to the custom of Moses, you cannot be saved.**" And when Paul and Barnabas had great dissension and debate with them, *the brethren* determined that Paul and Barnabas and some other of them should go up to Jerusalem to the apostles and elders concerning this issue.
> —Acts 15:1-2 (Italics original in NASB 95. Bolded for emphasis.)

---

was not the cause of eschatological salvation. The Mishna underscores the sins and unrighteousness of the people of Israel, but that, despite those sins, the people of Israel were nonetheless granted gracious acceptance into the kingdom. Therefore, historically speaking, in Pharisaical Judaism, there could have already been a tradition of being saved by grace, not by works. The fault, however, seems to be that this grace was exclusionary and only directed toward Israel, hence the need for Gentiles to become Jewish through proselytization.

The issue and context of Acts 15 is whether or not someone who was not a Jew and not circumcised could be saved. As shown above, based on first-century *theological* understanding, anyone wanting to be saved would have to become Jewish through some form of proselyte ceremony. In fact, since the time of the Maccabees, it seems that circumcision was the life-or-death marker of covenant inclusion. In other words, it was the only sure way one could know if someone was fully dedicated to the God of Israel. The requirement for correct circumcision was so ingrained that even if one wanted to switch sects of Judaism, say from a Sadducee to an Essene, they would undergo a new ceremony to conform to the *halacha* of the sect being joined. Interestingly, in the written Torah of Moses, unlike the prevailing customs, one will find no mention of a proselyte ceremony for non-Jews to become Jewish, nor any requirement of circumcision to secure a place in the resurrection. Yet, at the same time, God commands, in the written Torah, that all males be circumcised as a sign of the Abrahamic covenant and commands circumcision to participate in the Passover. This is undoubtedly the source of the confusion among the Judaisms and highlights why Paul and Barnabas's understanding of the timing of circumcision is important for correctly interpreting the command of circumcision for Gentiles.

The question that presented itself to the apostles was whether or not the status of the flesh guaranteed salvation. Paul, Barnabas, James, and Peter agreed that salvation is granted by faith, not due to the status of the flesh nor Jewish ethnicity. The reason they come to this conclusion is that, according to the Torah, Abraham believed first, and the command of circumcision came *after* his being declared righteous and his being saved by grace through faith (Gen. 15:6; Heb. 11:8-9, 17; Rom. 4:10). Genesis 15 shows—and Paul reiterates this point in Romans 4:10—that the promise and Abraham's faith were *before* his circumcision. Why? So that Abraham could be the father of both the circumcision (the physical lineage of Abraham) and the uncircumcision (Gentiles, who by faith are adopted as sons of Abraham). Thus, all nations and ethnicities, not just the Jews, could be blessed through Abraham. If everyone is required to become Jewish, as the prevailing belief in the first century held, then only one nation would receive the blessing, which clearly contradicts God's promise to Abraham. Again, this fundamental doctrine marked the main distinction between the new Jewish sect of "The Way" and the other sects of Judaism as well as the Judaizing Gentiles at the time.[37] One could even say this was an internal doctrinal battle *within* Judaism, or perhaps a struggle for who controlled the meaning of what Judaism was. The battle, it seems, was between the evolutionary Judaism and traditions that developed since the Maccabean era and the Messianic definition of the covenants. The Judaism and laws of the Pharisees originated from the Maccabean era in the 160s BC and other ancient forms of Judaism that emerged after Ezra and Nehemiah in the 600s BC. In contrast, the Messianic understanding is far older, stemming all the way back to Moses and Abraham. If the battle is for proper practice of Judaism, then it is certainly not a transition to a new religion as the transitory theory posits. Rather it is a return to a preexisting covenant. To use an anachronistic word from the Reformation, this seems to be an ancient form of *ad fontes*! Ultimately, this doctrine of Christ and the apostles was not a transitory avenue to a new belief, but rather a *reorientation* toward *preexisting* and perpetual truth based on the Abrahamic Covenant, the earliest faith.

---

37   A common interpretation based on supersessionist hermeneutics labels any Gentile who follows Torah commandments as a Judaizer. However, Judaizing specifically refers to Gentiles who take on the yoke of circumcision to become Jewish in order to ensure salvation.

The Apostles did not create or transition to a new soteriology in light of Christ; rather, they demonstrated that faith had always been the basis of the existing and irrevocable covenants (Heb. 11). In other words, Christ and the apostles are calling for a return to the faith of Abraham, for he is the father of us all (Jn. 8:39).

In this regard, it seems that Paul and Barnabas, along with the others of the council, held to a strict legal interpretation of circumcision. Here, it is quite important to understand what the Law says about circumcision. Circumcision was given to Abraham and *to all within his house*. In Genesis 17 it is written that all males born to Abraham, all servants *purchased with money*, and all the children of servants shall be circumcised. Legally speaking, this instance of mandatory childhood circumcision applied only to those born within the house of Abraham and those of Abraham's house who were purchased with money. Thus, circumcision is required only for babies who are eight days old and those purchased with money. Furthermore, the Torah details that Abram was called a Hebrew *before* his circumcision (Gen. 14:13). Therefore, it was not his circumcision that altered his ethnicity.[38]

The second requirement for circumcision comes from Exodus 12 and is applicable for both direct descendants from Israel and Gentiles when it comes to the *observation of the Passover*. Exodus 12:42 indicates

---

38   The identification as a Hebrew continues all the way through the time of the apostles. Acts 6:1 is particularly interesting in that it recognizes a socio-religious distinction between native Hebrews and Hellenistic Jews. While there is some debate as to whether these Hellenistic Jews were Gentiles who adopted Judaism or actually irreligious Jews who had not been circumcised and had adopted a Greek culture through assimilation, the latter seems to have a bit more support, as there were numerous communities of irreligious Jews around the Decapolis and the Nabatean areas east of the Jordan River. See Craig Keener, *Galatians: A Commentary* (Grand Rapids, MI: Baker Academic, 2019), 95-96.

that the Passover is a day set apart for Adonai that commemorates the redemption of Israel from the land of Egypt. Automatically, one can rule out that this observation and its requirements have any soteriological value whatsoever. Exodus 12:43-44 repeat the Abrahamic commands, and then verses 48-49 detail a new requirement for strangers and sojourners, should *they choose* to celebrate the Passover. It states that they must be circumcised.[39] While the LXX translates the Hebrew term *ger* as *proselytos*, the context suggests that, whatever this type of proselyte referred to, it differed from the first-century proselyte ceremony, as the meaning of the word was still evolving within Judaism at that time.[40] The context of Exodus 12 indicates that these individuals had not yet been circumcised but had decided they wanted to observe this Holy Day. If they were proselytes according to the traditions of the first century, then there would be no need for the injunction of circumcision since that would have already been taken care of in the proselyte ceremony. At the end of the day, however, what the Torah specifically requires for circumcision is not for *soteriological purposes* but for Gentiles who wanted to observe the rites of Passover. For the sons of Abraham, circumcision was the sign of the covenant by which the promised seed would come. Though, since the time of the Maccabees, this sign simply became a social identifier and a delineation between

---

39 A circumcision mandated by the Word of Adonai is certainly in a different category than a law made by a mere man which demands the following of oral tradition in order to have social and epistemic proof of salvation and covenant inclusion. In other words, only God can demand circumcision from individuals like he did with Abraham and with the son of Moses (Ex. 4:25).

40 Kuhn notes that the final development of "proselyte" as a technical term to denote the Gentile who becomes a *full Jew by circumcision* irrespective of his national or social position did not take place in Palestinian Judaism but in the Judaism of the Graeco-Roman diaspora." (Italics for emphasis). Kuhn, "προσήλυτος" in TDNT, 6:730.

those defiled by idols and the people of Adonai.[41] With this physical circumcision, there ought to have been a direct association with an internal state (circumcision of the heart), which marked true faith in the promises and gospel spoken to Abraham.[42] As for Gentiles, should they desire to undergo a circumcision to observe Passover and draw nearer to God by observing and celebrating the historical confirmation of the prophesy given to Abraham, they have, for all intents and purposes, *already* put their trust into the God of Israel. Considering the severe social cost that a Gentile would incur with this circumcision, it seems that only those who truly and willingly wanted to would pursue these commands.[43] With that being said, what one should notice right away is that the circumcision is done on one's own volition and there is no forced circumcision that is associated with the command. The whole notion of *forced* circumcision *for salvation* is precisely the issue presented in Acts 15:1 and in Galatians 2:3; 6:12. But as we have seen, there is no commandment in the Torah for forced *adult* circumcision. Legally speaking, biblical *adult* circumcision is for those who are foreigners who have joined themselves to Abraham and who want to walk in the *commandment of Passover*.[44] This stands in opposition to any oral

---

41   Craig S. Keener, *Galatians: A Commentary* (Baker Academic, 2019), 84.

42   Gal. 3:8.; Gen. 18:18; 26:4.; Deut. 10:16; 30:6; Lev. 26:41; Jer. 4:4; 9:25-26; Ez. 44:7, 9.

43   It is imperative to know that both Greek and Roman societies viewed the Jewish rite of proselyte circumcision as an overt and unrepealable repudiation of the gods and thus almost all aspects of civil society.

44   In addition to this, it seems that the Passover commands (with its sacrificial accoutrement) can only be truly fulfilled in the location where God has placed his Name, whether in Jerusalem or wherever the Tabernacle was during the Exodus journey. This does not mean, however, that one cannot observe the Passover in the diaspora. Here I am making a distinction between observance of the Passover and the Feast of Unleavened Bread, and actually fulfilling the law regarding Passover. The case can be made that observance of the day while being too far away from the Temple or too poor to make the journey is

law requiring circumcision for the purpose of changing ethnicity or for inclusion in salvation.[45]

Therefore, it would be decidedly against the Law for Gentiles to participate in a proselyte ceremony for salvation because the circumcision would not have been done at the right time or for the right reasons.[46] Furthermore, since adult Gentile believers are not purchased with money but with blood, they do not fit the criteria for circumcision detailed in Genesis 17, even though they are adopted into the family of Abraham (Acts 20:28; Eph. 2:15; Gal. 3:8). Given that Gentile inclusion into the family of Abraham is by the blood of Christ and not by the exchange of money, the requirement for ethnic conversion for salvation is moot. What is more, the laws for ethnic conversion are rooted in man-made traditions. A proselyte ceremony based on Pharisaical law is clearly not the same as the Law established by the Master of the Universe—the Law that Paul, Barnabas, and the First Jerusalem Council were committed to upholding.[47]

Now that we have established the legal grounds for circumcision, as it was interpreted by the First Jerusalem Council, we can now

---

different than fully walking in the command (i.e., Deut. 12:21). Given that the sacrifice could only be performed in Jerusalem or at the Temple, there is a sense in which the requirement for circumcision might only be fully applicable if a male and his family wanted to fulfill the requirements which depend on a Temple or Mishkan structure at a particular location (that being in the Land). Daniel's actions during the Babylonian exile illustrate the attitude. Daniel observed the sacrifice times by praying three times daily toward Jerusalem. Here he observed the required sacrifice times even though he was not actually able to fulfill the sacrifice. Likewise, Polycarp and Polycrates observed 14 Nisan, without the sacrificial service.

45   Mark Nanos, "Paul's Non-Jews Do Not Become 'Jews,' But Do they Become 'Jewish'?: Reading Romans 2:25-29 Within Judaism, Alongside Josephus, " *JJMJS* 1 (2014), 51.

46   Thiessen, *The Gentile Problem*, 67-68; 78-82.

47   Acts 15:21 "Moses is preached..."

move on to discussing the Transitory Theory in relation to circumcision. Although most commentators argue that God has "redefined" or transitioned away from a requirement of physical circumcision to a spiritual circumcision of the heart through faith and baptism—an interpretation largely based on their (mis)reading of Galatians and supersessionist assumptions dating back to early apologists like Irenaeus and Origen—there is a growing body of evidence suggesting that no such transition has occurred.[48] For one thing, circumcision of the heart has a long history in ancient Jewish thought. When the idea of heart-circumcision is presented in the biblical literature, it does not seem to be presented as a polemic against physical circumcision.[49] Rather, within faithful Judaism, it seems that there was always an expectation of hidden personal piety and faith in the coming Messiah, which was supposed to be the marker of a what a true covenant member was. This type of piety was taught by Christ and is not new within Judaism (Mt. 6:1-24). To that end, Hebrews 11 demonstrates that Abraham, Moses, and others had this faith and demonstrated this internal piety by faith. By the first century, however, it seems that many of the truly pious champions of the Abrahamic and Mosaic covenants had lost their way and had developed a religion of laws contained in ordinances that stood counter to the commands of God.[50] Given this

---

48 N.T. Wright, *Paul and the Faithfulness of God* (Fortress Press, 2013), 920-921; Collman, "(Un)Making a Theological Mountain Out of a Cardiological Mohel: Heart-Circumcision in Paul's Epistles," *JJMJS* 10 (2023), 91.

49 Deut. 10:16; 30:6; Lev. 26:41; Jer. 4:4; 9:25-26; Ez. 44:7, 9. In the Qumran scrolls and other writings, the theme of circumcision of the heart is found in 1QPHab 11.13; 4Q434 Frag. 1, 1.4; Jub. 1:23; Odes of Solomon 11.1-3; Philo, *Spec.* 1.304-5; QG 3.46; cf. 1QS 5.5). Collman, "(Un)Making a Theological Mountain Out of a Cardiological Mohel: Heart-Circumcision in Paul's Epistles," *JJMJS* 10 (2023), 101.

50 Mk. 7:1-13.; Among those who were indeed righteous and seeking the kingdom are Mary and Joseph (Mt. 1:19), John the Immerser, and Nathanael (Jn. 1:47) D.G. Dunn,

cultural context, Christ had come to accurately interpret the covenants and bring correction and repentance to everyone.[51] Accordingly, the apostles were the ones tasked with teaching what the Messiah taught regarding Gentile inclusion into the covenants of the Promise (Mt. 28:19; Acts 13:47).

Given the soteriological understanding of first-century Pharisaical Judaism, interpreters are required to make a distinction between the commandments of God for circumcision and the commandments of men that required circumcision. This is the very scenario that confronted the First Jerusalem Council and Paul at Galatia. Now, if there is a distinction between the Law of God and the law of Men, and the Scriptural data inclines me to think there is, this brings up the curious case study and distinction between Titus and Timothy and what Paul could have meant in 1 Corinthians 7:19-20. If Galatians was written before the First Jerusalem Council, this would mean that Paul thought that it was good for Timothy to be circumcised, even after Paul's supposedly anti-circumcision message to the Gentiles (Acts 16:3).[52] (Timothy would have been considered a Gentile, "for they [the Jews] all knew that his father was a Greek.") Although some Christian commentators attempt to say that Timothy was a Jew given the status of his Jewish mother, this is decidedly anachronistic, for at this time in Jewish

---

Epistle to the Galatians, ed. Henry Chadwick (Baker Academic, 1993), 136; N.T. Wright, *Justification: God's Plan and Paul's Vision* (IVP Academic, 2009), 146.

51 Mt. 5:17-19; Eph. 2:14-15.; Knox Chamblin, "Law of Moses and the Law of Christ," in *Continuity and Discontinuity: Perspectives on the Relationship Between the Old and New Testaments*, ed. John S. Feinberg, (Crossway, 1988), 191.

52 Moises Silva, *Interpreting Galatians* (Grand Rapids, MI: Baker, 2001), 131-132.; J.B. Lightfoot, *St. Paul's Epistle to the Galatians* (Warren Draper, 1870), 58-61. http://www.classicchristianlibrary.org/library/lightfoot_jb/Lightfoot-Gal.pdf (Accessed April 2, 2024).

history, it was only the patristic lineage that was counted towards one's Jewish status.[53] What is more, the Tanakh typically presents heritage in patristic format. To that end, the addition of maternal lineage was a response to persecution, death, and a crisis of Jewish identity after the destruction of the Temple and most likely around the second century.[54] Given that Timothy's father was a Greek—and everyone knew it—his circumcision was all the more scandalous, both to Jews of the day and to modern interpreters. However, even if Galatians was written after the First Jerusalem Council, we have Paul circumcising a Gentile male, thus adding a supposedly unnecessary burden or an unbearable yoke. In both cases, the circumcision of Timothy is a theological issue for Pauline interpretation. Given this obvious issue after the First Jerusalem Council, some commentators like Tenney resort to transitory explanations for this supposed lapse in Paul's judgment.[55] They make the case that Paul's doctrine was still developing, and Paul simply succumbed to his old Pharisaical "works of the law" in relationship to Timothy, but then came to his senses with Titus. As for Titus, all we actually know from Galatians 2:3 is that he was not *compelled* to undergo circumcision (see also Gal. 6:12). This means that Titus was not forced to undergo proselyte conversion according to the theological and Jewish legal understanding of the day.[56] What the text does *not* say is that Paul is denying the continued existence of the laws regarding circumcision found in the written Torah of God.[57] Furthermore,

---

53   Shaye J.D. Cohen, "Was Timothy Jewish? Acts 16:1-3," *JBL* 105, no. 2 (1986), 251-268.

54   Shaye J.D. Cohen, "The Origins of the Matrilineal Principle in Rabbinic Law," *AJS Review* 10, no.1 (Spring 1985), 19-53.

55   Merrill C. Tenney, *New Testament Survey Revised*, Revised by Walter M. Dunnett (Eerdmans, 1985), 246-255.

56   Hegg, *Galatians*, 61-63; Cha, *Misunderstanding Galatians*, 84.

57   *Shabbat* 31a.

Paul is *not* denying that Titus might want to undergo circumcision at a later date to fully observe a Passover, having been taught what the Law said regarding it (Acts 15:21; 1 Cor. 11:2; 2 Thess. 2:15). If this is the case, then a potential explanation for Timothy's circumcision was that he was mature enough in the faith, having heard the Law of Moses every Sabbath (Acts 15:21), and that he was under no compulsion to perform proselyte ceremonial circumcision.[58] From this line of reasoning, we can conclude that if what truly matters is keeping God's commandments (1 Cor. 7:19), Paul is not opposing the commandments concerning circumcision. Instead, he is rejecting the idea that circumcision, as practiced under Jewish oral tradition, can earn or merit positional justification and covenant membership.[59] To that end, those holding to the transitory understanding regarding the circumcision of Timothy and Titus typically use 1 Cor. 7:19-20 as proof that any Gentile circumcision is in some way Judaizing, but the scriptural evidence makes no mention of Timothy becoming ethnically Jewish, and he most certainly wasn't circumcised for salvific purposes.

Given what has been covered so far, it must be emphasized here that "Judaizing" can only really be defined as those Gentiles who have taken the yoke of *proselyte circumcision and Pharisaical oral law* upon themselves. These same Gentiles were the ones coercing other Gentiles and teaching that they could not be saved unless they underwent proselyte circumcision (Acts 15:1). Based on this understanding, the best way to interpret 1 Corinthians 7:18-20 is that Gentiles are not to undergo a *proselyte circumcision*. The key verse is verse 19: "Circumcision is nothing, and uncircumcision is nothing, but keeping/

---

58 Based on Galatians, compulsion seems to be the only difference between Timothy and Titus (Gal. 2:3; 6:12).

59 Cha, *Misunderstanding Galatians*, 83-84.

guarding the commandments of God."[60] This stands to interpret verse 18, which says, "Is any man called being circumcised? Let him not become uncircumcised. Is any called in uncircumcision? Let him not be circumcised." If circumcision is nothing, but the guarding and complying with the commands of God is what Paul wants to emphasize, then Paul's use of "circumcision" seems to be shorthand for proselyte circumcision (ethnic conversion) and not the commands of God regarding circumcision. The phrase "each one must remain in the way they were called" in verse 20, therefore, can be understood as referring to their *ethnic status*.[61] Gentiles cannot become native Jews and Jews should definitely not perform *epispasm* to regrow their foreskin in order to become "Gentiles" for social convenience in the Greek-dominated areas. Each one is to remain what they are, for there is no distinction between Jew and Greek, but all that matters is following the commandments of God. Here, Paul is holding to a stringent interpretation of the Torah. As covered earlier, Gentile circumcision in Exodus 12 does not confer a new ethnicity to the foreigner—rather, the foreigner remains

---

60   *Teresis* has a notion of a prison guard. In its other two uses in the NT it is used in connection with the apostles being arrested (Acts 4:3; 5:18). Here Paul is emphasizing a radical adherence to the commandments of God, keeping them under lock and key, the way a faithful guard would watch those in his custody. Some interpretations add an additional phrase to this verse adding, "but what matters is keeping the commandments of God."

61   Like Caleb (Num 13:6, 30; Josh. 14), one must remain in the way they were called (no proselyte circumcision, no cultural or forced epispasm). If Jewish persecution and economic participation was in view with Paul's writing, then like the time of the Maccabees there was significant cultural pressure to be uncircumcised for economic and social participation. This was eventually magnified after 70AD and most certainty by the persecution of Hadrian. Robert G. Hall, "Epispasm: Circumcision in Reverse," *Bible Review* (Aug. 1992), 52-57. https://www.cirp.org/library/restoration/hall1/ (Accessed January 4, 2023).

a foreigner. As it is written, there is one law for the foreigner and the native born if *the foreigner* wants to observe the Passover.[62]

The text of Exodus 12 does not specify when this circumcision was to take place. All that the Torah specifies is that the circumcision is to be complete before the Passover ceremony. Therefore, Timothy could have performed the circumcision at any time during the year because he set it in his heart to perform the Passover during the next year. Under the direction and supervision of Paul, Timothy, having been sanctified by the word of God, being free from compulsion, and wanting to do it for the right reasons, is circumcised as a Gentile. What is more is that this is done after the First Jerusalem Council and probably after the writing of Galatians.

Assuming a premillennial eschatologically, the continuity of circumcision is of particular interest for Gentiles and seems to parallel the circumcision of both foreigners and native born in Joshua 5. Ezekiel 44:9 says, "Thus says the Lord GOD: No foreigner, uncircumcised in heart and flesh, of all the foreigners who are among the people of Israel, shall enter my sanctuary." The command of Adonai is very clear here: any foreigner among the people of Israel will be circumcised *to enter the sanctuary*. To preclude a mere allegorical interpretation, the text requires both physical and spiritual circumcision! Who is the one

---

62 Perhaps Paul could also be making a point that for all intents and purposes, the Laws regarding circumcision, although completely relevant and current, are practically moot for many of the Gentiles in Corinth. How likely is it that these Gentiles, or even Jews living in Corinth, are actually going to make the journey to Israel to fulfill the Passover or any feast? Since Gentiles can participate in essentially everything but Passover, and the Passover ceremonies can only be fulfilled while in the land, in the context of Corinth, circumcision really does not mean too much as a practical matter. Corinth was over 700 nautical miles and 1,826 miles (2,940 km) by land to Jerusalem. Thus, they would only be observing the Passover.

that can judge the heart? Adonai. The text is quite specific, too: only those approaching and entering the sanctuary are to be circumcised. This person still retains their ethnic status as a "foreigner" but is commanded by Adonai to be physically circumcised and to show internal faithfulness to the covenants in order to approach. What should be clear is that Adonai alone, via his word, is able to mandate circumcision and when it should be performed.

Therefore, instead of revealing an evolutionary or transitory track in Paul's understanding of circumcision, the Scriptures actually present a strict adherence to the Law's commands and a clear contrast to the prevailing views of first-century Pharisaical Judaism and the "Judaism" of Gentile Judaizers. The case study of the First Jerusalem Council, the circumcision of Timothy, the (possibly) delayed circumcision of Titus, and the eschatological existence of Ezekiel's Temple, all demonstrate that Paul and the other apostles were not developing new doctrine or guessing at what the Holy Spirit wanted. Rather, they were following what the word of God says exactly—one might say to the letter and to the Spirit. Their interaction with the Party of the Circumcision, paganism, and other Jewish oral laws is a battle for correct and lawful doctrine based only on the word of God, which stands in stark contrast to the word of man.

But Isn't the Torah An Impossible Burden?: Do Peter's Words in Acts 15 Show Transition?

A common historical interpretation of Acts 15 by the those holding to the transitory and conciliatory theories is that the Mosaic Law was an impossible burden to bear. According to this view, a transition was needed because the Law was intentionally designed to be too difficult to follow.[63] This interpretation comes from Peter's words in Acts 15:10-11. It is argued that Peter is saying that the *written* Torah of God was a yoke that "neither our fathers nor we have been able to bear." The problem with this interpretation, as shown above, is that the historical and contextually accurate view is that salvation was already viewed as graciously granted to Israel as a people, and that perfect observation of the Torah was not the basis of eschatological salvation. Secondly, the text in Acts 15 has no mention of salvation by total perfect observation of the Law of God. Rather, the whole context in Acts 15 is about a *single facet* of the written Law (circumcision) and associated tradition (proselyte ceremony). In short, no one in the biblical text is actually discussing salvation by perfect and complete works of the Torah. In fact, the whole notion for the Jews, as Stendahl obverses, is that "the Law did not require a static or pedantic perfectionism but supposed a covenant relationship in which there was room for forgiveness and repentance."[64] Given this context and the actual covenantal relationship being spoken of, the main contention

---

63   It seems illogical to simultaneously say that during the dispensation of the Law, salvation was granted by works of the Law and also that the Law was too difficult to follow. The results of this type of double-minded thinking is that no one was actually saved during the dispensation of the Law, for it was too hard. The same position typically also holds that the Law of Christ is actually harder than the Law of Moses because of the supposedly added spiritual commands of not even thinking lustfully, while at the same time saying that the Law of Christ is easy and light. On both sides, the Law is too hard when both the Law of God and the Law of Christ are within reach and not too difficult. This position, besides being self-defeating, certainly opens up the charge of God being a cosmic sadist.

64   Krister Stendahl, "The Apostle Paul and the Introspective Conscience of the West," *Harvard Theological Review* 56.3 (July 1963), 201. Quote originally found in M.I. Cha, *Misunderstanding Galatians*, 6.

being discussed in Acts 15 is the coerced circumcision taught by those holding to Pharisaical oral law.[65]

Therefore, if it was generally assumed among 1st Century Judaisms that perfect observation of the Law was not required for salvation (as that salvation was already graciously granted), then what yoke is Peter talking about? For Moses, who was inspired by the Holy Spirit to write the words of the Torah, clearly indicates that the Law is *not too difficult* and that it is within reach (Deut. 30:11).[66] Shall I apply C.S. Lewis's method to Moses as done to Paul? *Aut Moses, aut malus homo.* Surely, Moses is not lying, here![67] Paul reinforces the idea that the Law is not too difficult through Christ by quoting Moses's declaration in Deuteronomy 30:11 and 14, emphasizing that the Law is within reach (Rom. 10:8). Most importantly, Christ is Adonai in the flesh, and he told us his yoke was "easy and light" (Mt. 11:30). Therefore, since Adonai gave the Torah, it must likewise be easy and light, which is simply confirmation of what Moses already wrote. Lastly, and philosophically speaking, if God made a yoke too difficult for humanity in general, or the Jews in particular, that simply makes him a cosmic sadist and an evil God.[68]

---

65 Avi ben Mordechai, *Galatians: A Torah Based Commentary in First-Century Hebraic Context* (Haifa: Millennium 7000 Communications, 2005), 173.

66 This ease of keeping the Law, of course, assumes faith first and a circumcised heart (Deut. 10:16; Deut. 30:6; Jer. 4:4; Heb. 11:23-29). In a New Covenant context, if one had the Spirit who wrote the Law on the heart, it would actually be easier to keep the Law with the Holy Spirit indwelling within the person. In other words, if Moses said it was not too difficult, it would be even easier to Peter and all those after the initiation of the New Covenant.

67 If Moses were to be lying, then the Holy Spirit who inspired him is also lying. This, of course, is devastating to biblical doctrine.

68 For more on this, see the section in my dissertation titled "In the Wake of Euthyphro's False Dilemma." See McKenzie, "Pronomian Paradigm" (Liberty University, 2024), 172-218.

So, it seems on several accounts that the burden Peter is speaking of is not the corpus of Moses but something else.[69]

Halacha and Dogmata: The Doctrines and Traditions of Men

If the Law of God is not the heavy and impossible yoke, then Peter must be referring to a different type of yoke—one found not in the written Torah but only in theology. In Acts 15:9-11, Peter's words indicate that the Jews and the Gentiles share the same faith and that there is no separation between them. Both groups are cleansed by their faith, not circumcision or any "works" of the Law. Peter is not saying that God's Law is an impossible yoke, but that it is powerless for the purpose of salvation, particularly when one relies on man-made laws to be made righteous. It is quite possible that Peter could also be speaking of works-based salvation here, based on halachic rules. Should Peter have Paul's words in Galatians in mind, if one tries to use circumcision and Law as a means of salvation, one will have to live totally and perfectly by the Law to achieve salvation, which is indeed a burden that no one can bear, for all have sinned and are under the curse of the Law. However, considering that most of Judaism thought perfect Torah observance was not the basis of salvation, this does not seem likely. Given the context of Gentiles coming into the community, it seems the burden that was impossible to bear refers to dogmatic barriers.[70] For if the dogma mandates that one must perform a work of circumcision for salvation, the whole work of the Law must be

---

69 As noted above, earning *salvation* by Torah is indeed an impossible burden because all have sinned and are under the curse of sin and death. But the Torah itself is not an impossible burden if pursued correctly.

70 Rob Vanhoff, "Circumcision in the Second Temple Period," Part 3, *Torah Resource* (2012), 2. https://tr-pdf.s3-us-west-2.amazonaws.com/articles/circumcision-in-the-second-temple-period.pdf (Accessed December 31, 2023).

performed for salvation. The nuance is that it started with a dogmatic barrier for covenant inclusion. If salvation is based on works of the Law, then it is a heavy yoke that is unbearable, but if the Law is practiced within grace already given, it is "easy and light." Therefore, the yoke that Peter must be speaking of is the *dogma* of proselyte salvation by circumcision, the rules and regulations that the various sects of Judaism have placed on the shoulders of converts. This is precisely what Christ said to the Pharisees and the Torah scholars in Matthew 23:4—"They time up heavy burdens and lay on men's shoulders, but they themselves are unwilling to move them with so much as a finger."

Again, here we see the apostles *reorientating* to *preexisting* and eternal truth and rejecting the halacha of first-century Judaism, which had become the unbearable yoke of requiring a work for the Gentiles to be saved. Christ also said to the Pharisees that even their halacha, some of which violated the Law of God, was actually making "sons of Gehenna" (Mt. 23:15). If the Pharisees were teaching that if a conversion to Judaism through circumcision saved them, and they had no real faith in the God of Israel, their discipleship under these Pharisees would most certainly turn them into a son of Gehenna. After all, a student is not greater than their teacher.

Therefore, what this passage indicates is that there is no transition away from the Law. Rather, in Acts 15, the apostles confirm that Moses is preached every Sabbath (Acts 15:21), and that they are reorienting toward preexisting truth and away from faulty teaching.[71]

---

71 Rabbinowitz, "Mt. 23:2-4," 446: "...Matthew presents 'Christian' Judaism as the only legitimate form of Judaism."

The Jew/Gentile Divide: Different Orthopraxy?

At the First Jerusalem Council, the apostles outlined four commands for new Gentile converts to follow. The common interpretation suggests that these converts were only required to adhere to these specific rules, but not the Law of Moses. This interpretation is linked to the context of the Second Jerusalem Council in Acts 21, where verse 21 explicitly refers to "Jews" and verse 25 mentions "Gentiles":

> And when they heard it they began glorifying God; and they said to him, 'You see, brother, how many thousands there are among the Jews of those who have believed, and they are all zealous for the Law; and they have been told about you, that you are teaching all the **Jews** who are among the Gentiles to forsake Moses, telling them not to circumcise their children nor to walk according to the customs.... But concerning the **Gentiles** who have believed, we wrote, having decided that they should abstain from meat sacrificed to idols and from blood and from what is strangled and from fornication.'
> —Acts 21:20-12, 25 (emphasis added)

In Acts 21, James is appealing to what was already written and decided at the First Jerusalem Council (Acts 15:19-21, 29). On the surgace, it appears that there is a clear distinction between the requirements for Jews and Gentiles—the Jews can continue keeping the law, while the Gentile converts simply have to keep the four requirements found in Acts 15. This separation—even though Peter said that there is no separation between Jew and Greek (Acts 15:9)—is usually explained by the conciliatory theory (i.e., being all things to all men), which will be explained in the next chapter. This section, however, is focused on the ruling issued at the First Jerusalem Council, which will show no *transition* in biblical doctrine.

As with all biblical passages, context is key. It is widely understood that first-century synagogues were mixed congregations, and Paul's epistles often address diverse audiences from various backgrounds.[72] In a synagogue, one might find believing Jews, believing Gentiles, and unbelieving Jews. This is evident from the opening verse of Acts 15, which indicates that both Gentiles and Jews were present in that particular synagogue. Some of these Jews (or even proselyte Gentiles) began teaching that circumcision was necessary for salvation, a view with which the Apostles obviously disagreed. The ruling in Acts 15, beginning in verse 19, shows that James, Paul, Peter, and John agreed on four dogmatic rules for the Gentiles.[73] Next, one must understand what is being discussed in Acts 15. These can be distilled into a few key points:

1. There was a disagreement on whether or not circumcision was *required for salvation.*

    a. Keep in mind the historical context of first-century Judaisms. It was vital to understand that there were different sects of Judaism at the time—Pharisee, Sadducee, Essene, and now also the sect of the Nazarenes. Paul himself identifies as both a Pharisee and the leader of the Nazarenes (Acts 24:5; 26:5; 28:22; Phil. 3:5). As has been stated several times already, a common (mis)understanding in first-century Judaism was that circumcision, and follow-

---

72 Mark Nanos, *The Mystery of Romans*, 76-84.; see also, A.J.M. Wedderburn, *The Reason for Romans* (Fortress Press,1991).

73 Acts 16:4 (*dogmata*).

ing other halakha was required for salvation and participation in the eschatological kingdom of God. Those who held this position had come to be known as the "Party of the Circumcision" here in Acts 15 and are probably the main antagonists of Paul (particularly in Galatians).

b. More specifically, the Party of the Circumcision thought that one had to become Jewish in order to partake in the covenants of the Promise. Thus, a conversion ceremony of circumcision was needed to ensure that new Gentiles made a total break from their idolatrous ways. It needs to be reemphasized that this ceremony cannot be found in the written Torah. It was a ceremony derived from *theology* and oral tradition, which was later codified in the Mishna and Talmud.

2. The apostles, interpreting the Abrahamic covenant, determine that the Party of the Circumcision is mistaken because Abraham was justified by faith before his circumcision (Rom. 4:11-12; Heb. 11:8-19).

3. The apostles rule that the Gentiles do not need to become Jewish by circumcision in order to participate in salvation and the eschatological kingdom. Salvation is based not on ethnicity, nor the status of one's foreskin. Salvation was granted in the same way it was granted to Abraham—by grace through faith.

4. However, in order for the Jews to be satisfied that the new Gentile converts would not be bringing in syncretic practices from the pagan temples and their unclean cultural practices, initial rules (Grk. *dogmata*) needed to be set in place for the Gentiles (Acts 16:4).

Again, it is important to keep the historical context in mind with the myriad of rules that the sages and rabbis had put on top of the people (the heavy burdens that Peter disparages in this same text; see also Matt. 11:30). So, Luke is recording a confluence of interrelated topics that are present in first-century Judaism. This is why it is vitally important to know the context, which is about the salvific effectiveness of circumcision and the means of Gentile inclusion, not the entire corpus of the Mosaic Law (nor the corpus of the Rabbinic halacha), as is commonly interpreted.

Dogma and the Written Rules of the Law in Acts 15

Verse 19 begins the detailing of the new dogma issued from the apostles: (1) abstain from things sacrificed to idols, (2) abstain from blood (most likely the ingesting of blood from the pagan sacrifice), (3) abstain from things strangled, (4) abstain from fornication, and (5) be in synagogue to hear Moses preached (Acts 15:21).[74] What one should immediately notice from the ruling is that the rules come from the Mosaic Law or are practical rules (dogma) for following specific Torah commands:

1. **Abstain from things sacrificed to idols.** This command is not specifically found in the Torah. This is a dogmatic ruling that follows the spirit of the letter. As the eating of meats

---

74 This is not explicitly mentioned in 15:29 where James summarizes the essential dogma, nor is it repeated in Acts 21. However, it is explicitly said in Act 15:21, and the context would make hearing the Law a given because the Gentiles would obviously be in a synagogue where Moses would naturally be heard. I have chosen to make this fifth command of the First Jerusalem Council visible. Thus, the first four commands are required to even be in association with the people of the synagogue. Wilber, *Remember the Sabbath*, 122.; Ariel and D'vorah Berkowitz, *Torah Rediscovered*, 70-71.

sacrificed to idols is participation in pagan worship and a violation of the first and second commandments, the Shema (Deut. 6:4-9), and the command to not learn the ways of the nations (Deut. 18:9) by worshiping God with pagan syncretism. Paul describes this as the table of demons (1 Cor. 10:21). It should be noted, however, that this sacrificial meat stands in contrast to that which might be sold in the marketplace. During this historical period, the marketplace in Greek-dominated areas was often within the temple precinct, but the meats contained therein are not necessarily a result of pagan temple slaughtering. Paul says that market meats are okay if one does not know its status and if one's conscience allows. Furthermore, if one knows or has been informed that said meat was sacrificed to idols, Paul says "do not eat" (1 Cor. 10:28). In 1 Corinthians 10, Paul refuses to add additional dogma, which would place a greater burden, but simply follows James's ruling to the letter in Acts 15.[75] Ultimately, although one could eat meats, if they were ignorant of the origins, it is better for one to give up that freedom for the sake of one who totally forsakes all marketplace meats.

2. **Abstain from blood.** This law is specifically found in the Torah (Lev. 3:17; 17:2). Adonai has forbidden the drinking or eating of blood. In the pagan temples, the ingesting of blood was commonly practiced as part of the rites.

---

75 The text of 1 Cor. 10 is often taken by the majority of commentators as speaking of unclean meats that have become okay to eat. But given the context, this is very unlikely. Rather, there was a dispute as to whether in the marketplace biblically clean meats were made unclean simply because of their proximity and the possibility of contamination from pagan temples. Paul's ruling is to abstain from unholy things (confirming Acts 15).

3. **Abstain from things strangled.** This command is not specifically found in the Torah, but is certainly connected to the command not to eat the blood. Given that most modern people have no knowledge of butchering techniques, it is easy to see why this command would be confusing. If one strangles an animal, none of the blood escapes, as the heart no longer pumps. The meat stays saturated with blood. This is why kosher killing practices (dogma) were developed, so that the blood is drained out. Furthermore, the strangulation of an animal causes severe stress for the animal. Simply put, it is inhumane. To place undue suffering on a creature is diametrically opposed to the spirit of the Torah and runs counter to the instructions given in Proverbs 12:10. A true man of the land and agriculture should never mistreat animals, even during the butchering process. Finally, and most importantly, to torture an animal for the sake of demon satisfaction shows a level of human depravity that can only be overshadowed by human sacrifice. Torture of animals is a violation of the creation mandate (Gen. 1:27-28), and to do it for an idol is simply abominable.

4. **Abstain from fornication.** This is another command found in the Torah. As it is written, "Do not commit adultery." Pagan temple prostitution is wrong, and sexual promiscuity on top of pagan worship is obviously against the entire biblical thrust of holy living. Furthermore, as already pointed out, apostasy is adultery.

5. **Observe the Sabbath.** This is not in verse 29, but is included in verse 21. The first four commands are the "essentials" that the apostles put in place for the Gentiles to even come into the synagogue in order to follow the fourth commandment of the

decalogue. Given the historical context, the new Gentile converts would be going to a synagogue where Moses is naturally preached. It seems reasonable to assume that Gentile converts were expected to be part of the community and would have attended the Sabbath gatherings, where they would naturally hear the reading of Moses and the Prophets. If Moses is read, then it was expected for Gentiles to hear and obey.[76]

The First Day of the Week Objection: An Excursus

At this point, a common objection to the traditional Sabbath is the belief that the day of worship and hearing the Law shifted from the biblical Sabbath, moving 24 hours later to Sunday. The transition to Sunday is buttressed with five interpretative maneuvers based on the following accounts: (1) The resurrection accounts in the Gospels, (2) Romans 14, (3) Acts 20:7-12, (4) 1 Corinthians 16:1-3, and (5) Colossians 2.

Regarding the resurrection accounts in the Gospels, this is perhaps the biggest evidence for those claiming a transition to Sunday. The problem is that most have failed to understand the Holy Days written about in the Tanakh, so they fail to understand the Holy Days described in the Tanakh, leading to a misunderstanding of the timing and broader context presented in Scripture concerning the death and resurrection of the Messiah. Although this section is not concerned with showing the chronology of the crucifixion and how the synoptics as well as John display a consistent timing of both the death and resurrection, this chapter is most interested in showing how Christ's death and resurrection follow an exact adherence to the Law

---

76   J.K. McKee, *The New Testament Validates Torah* (Richardson, TX: Messianic Apologetics, 2012), 86.

of Moses, not transitioning away from it.[77] In 30AD, the Passover was on a Thursday (14 Nisan/April 6) and the sighting of the crescent moon on 1 Nisan/March 24.[78] This would mean that the beginning of the counting of the Omer for Shavuot/Pentecost (Feast of Weeks) would begin on Sunday (17 Nisan). The resurrection accounts indicate that Christ rose sometime after the Sabbath ended, but before dawn on the third day. This day is indeed a "Sunday," but in the rush to see a mere Sunday—and thus a transition away from the Sabbath—the majority actually miss the target, which is that Christ rose on the first day of the first fruits season proclaimed in the Law of Moses during the Feast of Unleavened Bread. This fact is not lost on the apostle Paul in 1 Corinthians 15:20. The fact is that "Sunday," the 17th of Nisan, was a crucial part of the biblical Feasts of Unleavened Bread and the Feast of Weeks. Rather than marking a transition to something new, as much of Church history claims, Christ's resurrection follows the ancient patterns established by Moses in the Word of God with miraculous precision.[79] Merely seeing a "Sunday" and assuming a required change

---

77 For an excellent overview of the Chronology and a study on how the synoptics and John can be synthesized into a cogent timeline (especially that the "Last Supper" was indeed a Passover meal), see Joachim Heremias, *The Eucharistic Words of Jesus* (Macmillin, 1955); Tim Hegg, "The Chronology of the Crucifixion: A Comparison of the Gospel Accounts," *Torah Resource* 2017.

78 It is important to note that Hebraic days are counted from sundown.

79 Although, the majority view today has by in large taken the view of Easter/Sunday, there was significant disagreement particularly between the Roman leaders and leaders in Asia Minor. But even the geographic difference can be debated, contra Eusebius who claims that churches, with the exception of churches in Asia Minor, celebrated Easter on Sunday (*Ecclesiastical History* 5.23.1), Bacchiocchi indicates that this supposed "heresy" was quite widespread and may have continued until the forced removal of circumcised bishops around 135AD. It is well known that both Polycarp and Polycrates, who claim to have had direct instruction from both John and Philip, refused to accept the edicts from the Roman Vicars regarding their celebration of Passover. See Bacchiochi, *From Sabbath*

is to miss the forest for the trees.[80] In fact, a true following of the scriptures would lead everyone to observe Passover and First Fruits in remembrance of Christ, rather than shifting to holidays that are not mentioned in the Tanakh. These later holidays primarily originated from the early, and often debated, development of Roman-centered theology in the second century.

Bacchiocchi says, "The role that the Church of Rome played in causing the abandonment of the Sabbath and the adoption of Sunday has been underestimated, if not totally neglected in recent studies."[81] The contested nature of the Sabbath, along with the shift to other holidays and different methods of timekeeping, suggests that it may not have been Scripture that mandated the change. Instead, it was likely the development of theology[82] and social pressures that drove the supposed

---

80 Eusebius writes in *De Solemnitate Paschali*, 7: "While the Jews faithful to Moses, sacrificed the Passover lamb once a year...we men of the New Covenant celebrate every Sunday our Passover." Even today, Italians recognize Sunday as "Pasquetta," which means "Little Easter."

81 Bacchiocchi, *From Sabbath to Sunday*, 211. I must give Bacchiocchi much praise in his work *Sabbath to Sunday*, as his work and research was indispensable in guiding my research on this topic, primarily in the identification of primary sources.

82 Theology is the result of method, hermeneutics, and assumptions. So, for instance, using Ignatius's hermeneutics as an example, in Magnesians, he attempts to show that it was the Prophets of the Tanakh that began the trend in "no longer Sabbatizing." According to Ignatius, since the Prophets lived in accordance with Jesus Christ (Magnesians 8:1-2), they were no longer Sabbatizing but living according to the Lord's life. This type of hermeneutics is not based on any actual historical nor a plain reading of the prophetic literature, but seems to be theologically derived, through a priori rejection of both the Sabbath and anything based on the Law. Is. 66:23 is one such example which go against Ignatius's view. Rather, Ignatius's hermeneutics seem to be from a deep-seated anti-Jewish bias developed from social, political, military, and economic pressures. See

transition to Sunday and Easter.[83] In fact, both Pagan and Christian sources denigrate the "superstitions" of the Jews as reasons why the Sabbath should be discouraged and even penalized.[84] From the time of Hadrian, a radical and repressive policy against the Jews was enacted and is spoken of in the Talmud that has eerie similarity to the tyranny that earlier Jews were exposed to during the time of the Maccabees.[85] As Bacchiocchi notes, where these social pressures (anti-Jewishness) were less influential, the observance of the Sabbath, Passover, and other

---

W.D. Davies, Christian Origins and Judaism (Arno Press, 1973, 74). Bruce Metzger, as quoted by Bacchiocchi, likewise shows that after the Jewish rebellion under Hadrian "... it became vitally important for those who were not Jews to avoid exposing themselves to suspicion; and the observance of the Sabbath was one of the most noticeable indications of Judaism. See Metzger, The Saturday and Sunday Lessons from Luke in the Greek Gospel Lectionary, Studies in the Lectionary Text of the Greek New Testament, Vol. 2, no. 3 (Chicago University Press, 1944), 12; quoted on Bacchiocchi, Sabbath to Sunday, 212.

83 See the Didascalia Apostolorum 21:17, which mandates the following of 14 Nisan. However, many, like Epiphanius, think that those who followed the Quartodeciman view were mistaken and that there should be unity by adopting Easter-Sunday, thus replacing 14 Nisan (See Adversus Haereses). What should be noted is that the transition from 14 Nisan and Sabbath did not really begin in earnest until after Hadrian's oppressive regime and the replacement of bishops who were viewed as Judaizing by following the Quartodeciman model. Didascalia Apostolorum, trans. Margaret Dunlop Gibson (Cambridge University Press, 1903). https://dn790004.ca.archive.org/0/items/didascaliaaposto00gibsuoft/didascaliaaposto00gibsuoft.pdf (Accessed April 8, 2024).

84 Plutarch, De Superstitione, section 8, http://www.perseus.tufts.edu/hopper/text?doc=Perseus%3Atext%3A2008.01.0190%3Asection%3D8 (Date accessed March 31, 2024). Early Christian sources attest to viewing the physical obedience to the Law as "superstitions." The Letter to Diognetus says, "superstitions as respects the Sabbaths." The same can be said for the writings of Justin (Dialouge with Trypho, 29.3) and Chyrsostom (De Christi Divinitate 4) as well as others such as Epiphanius (Adversus Haereses).

85 Rosh Hashanah 19a.; Baba Bathra 60b.

Moedim was much more common, particularly in Asia Minor and sur-rounding Israel, as shown by the writings of Epiphanius and Eusebius.

A very potent case study, masterfully done by Ray Pritz, in his book *Nazarene Jewish Christianity*, details an example of this bifurcation in historical Christianity with the history of the Sect of the Nazarene.[86] Interestingly, Pritz found within these early writings in the second through fourth century—particularly those of Eusebius, Epiphanius, and Jerome—a sect of Law-keeping Christians of Jewish background.[87] From these writings in ecclesiastical history, clues begin to emerge of a very early sect formed just after the resurrection, based in Jerusa-lem, and directly connected to the earliest Church led by James (Acts 21). These people eventually fled to Pella (70 AD) and then began disappearing or were persecuted to death sometime around the fourth century.[88] Pritz details that the Sect of the Nazarenes was actually con-fused by several of the early Church apologists as either Ebionites or other heretical offshoots. Pritz, however, makes the point that these believers had several doctrinal factors, primarily their Christology and their acceptance of Paul as conforming to much of the orthodoxy forming in Rome starting with Ignatius and Irenaeus.[89] Primarily, they had a basically trinitarian view, they accepted the virgin birth, they

---

86   Ray A. Pritz, *Nazarene Jewish Christianity* (Hebrew University Press, 2006).

87   Ibid., 108.

88   Ibid., 10. The evidence as presented by Bacchiocchi, Davies, Metzger, Kaiser, Nanos, and others seems to indicate that persecution has come from three sources: (1) Unbelieving Jews, who no doubt began to expel those in the Jesus Movement out of their synagogues (see D. Thomas Lancaster, *From Sabbath to Sabbath: Returning the Holy Sabbath to the Disciples of Jesus* [Marshfield, MO: First Fruits of Zion, 2016], 257), (2) pagans who regarded any form of Jewish practice, primarily circumcision and rejection of cultural idolatry, as reasons to consider people *persona non grata*, and (3) Roman Christians who view any form of obedience to the Law of God as "Superstitions" and "Judaizing."

89   The Earlier Polycarp maintained at least observance of the Passover as shown above.

---

accepted the divinity of Yeshua, they had a growing doctrine of the Holy Spirit, they did not reject Paul, and they accepted Gentiles. What is quite interesting is that even the most ardent of the fourth-century "fathers" could find no real fault with this group. Quoting M. Simon, Bacchiocchi writes that the Nazarenes "are characterized essentially by their tenacious attachment to Jewish observances. If they became heretics in the eyes of the Mother church, it is simply because they *remained fixed on outmoded positions*. They well represent…the very direct descendants of the *primitive community*, of which our author knows that it was designated by the Jews by the same name of Nazarenes."[90] In other words, Epiphanius and others can find no fault with the Nazarenes in Christology or other areas of potential "heresy," save that they observed what was now considered "outmoded."[91] The main contention that the leaders in Rome had with the Sect of the Nazarenes was praxis and insistence on Mosaic continuity, including childhood circumcision, the Sabbath, and the moedim.[92]

Further substantiating this view is that the Didache seems to point to the "Lord's Day" being the Sabbath. Didache 14:1-2 says, "On the Lord's own day, when you gather together, break bread and give thanks [Or: celebrate the eucharist] after you have confessed your unlawful deeds, that your sacrifice may be pure. Let no one quarreling with his neighbor join you until they are reconciled, that your sacrifice may

---

90   Bacchiocchi, *From Sabbath to Sunday*, 156. Emphasis added.

91   See Epiphanius, *Adversus Haereses*, 29, 7. As to how the Word of God can become "outmoded" in any form or fashion seems to be negated by Paul's own insistence that the Tankah is good for teaching, reproof, correction, and training in righteousness" (2 Tim. 3:16).

92   Pritz, *Nazarene Jewish Christianity*, 109. The Laws about circumcision were discussed earlier in this book, and it was shown that no scriptural transition can be found.

not be defiled."[93] Perhaps, if one considers that Christ himself said he is "Lord of the Sabbath," that the "Lord's own day" could actually be referring to the Sabbath instead of being *assumed* as Sunday. Historically, as Bacchiocchi demonstrates, Sunday worship did not become common until later in the second century, thus making the interpretation that the Didache refers to Sunday worship anachronistic.[94] What is more, internal evidence within the Didache itself mentions "preparation day" (Didache 8:1), which is the traditional designation for Friday.[95] Therefore, the assumption that "Lord's own day" in the Didache must mean Sunday does not necessarily follow, for the evidence, both scripturally and internally, have significant markers toward the Sabbath. The question that presents itself is, when did the Sabbath become "outmoded" because neither Scripture nor the earlier Christian writings seem to indicate the Sabbath as "outmoded." Rather, observance of the Sabbath seemed to be a common and continuous marker for the believers in the first century.

Therefore, given the extremely early origins of this group of Jewish Christians, which stem back to the teaching of James, there is significant historical grounds to consider the Sect of the Nazarenes as the gold standard in historical orthopraxy and orthodoxy. Contra the claims of a universal belief and proper practice as proclaimed by many of the leaders in Rome, the Jewish and Gentile congregations in earlier Christianity, particularly the sects of Christianity with direct ties to the earliest believers in Asia Minor and Palestine, maintained a significant orthopraxy tied to the Mosaic Law, as opposed to emerging cultural

---

93   From Bart D. Ehrman, *The Apostolic Fathers*, vol. 1, 439.

94   Mt. 12:8; Mk. 2:28; Lk 6:5. Bacchiocchi, *From Sabbath to Sunday*, 198-212.

95   Mt. 27:62; Mk. 15:42; Lk. 23:54; Jn. 19:14; Josephus, *Antiquities* 16:163. παρασκευήν is translated as "Friday" in most English translations, but more commonly means "preparation day."

and political influences that were much more pronounced in Rome, especially during the reign of Hadrian. In closing this section, what the Scriptures present is Christ commanding, "Do this in remembrance of me." The "this" is the Passover, and everything associated with the timing of the Passover and associated feasts of Unleavened Bread and Shavuot (Pentecost) can only be accomplished by calculations of the Sabbaths biblically. Therefore, there is no biblically mandated transition from Sabbath to Sunday found in the resurrection accounts.[96] History and literal hermeneutics show that this transition is not explicitly found in scripture, but is only found through theological additions. Whether this shift was intentional or not is irrelevant, but like Purim or Hanukkah, this additional celebration of the resurrection, which was likely on a Sunday, probably began as a once a year occurrence during the Feast of Unleavened Bread.[97] However, this additional celebration actually corresponds to an already existing day for the beginning of the "First Fruits" Omer count, so there was not really an additional celebration created, rather, its Messianic implications became fully manifested.[98] Over time, this additional day became the dominant day through social, religious, and economic pressure.[99] In short, Sunday worship is

---

96 J.C. Laansma says, "There is no indication in the NT evidence that the day (Sunday) displaced or rivaled the Sabbath, that it was a day of rest, that it had anything to do with the Fourth Commandment or that it involved any sort of transfer theology." Laansma, "The Lord's Day" in *The Dictionary of the Later New Testament and Its Developments* (IVP, 1997), 683.

97 Bacchiocchi, *From Sabbath to Sunday*, 204-207.

98 Ex. 23:16; Lev. 23:15-17. This is not lost on the Apostle Paul, who says Christ is the first fruits from the dead. 1 Cor. 15:23.

99 It is my opinion that Paul even recognized the potential social, political, economic, and military context which could cause a bifurcation like the transition from Sabbath to Sunday. Romans 13 can be interpreted as an effort to ensure that new Gentile converts would continue to identify with their Jewish brothers. For example, Gentiles should pay

tradition that cannot be substantiated via the resurrection accounts but was a developmental and societal/political creation steeped in anti-Judaic rhetoric.[100]

Regarding the supposed transition in Romans 14, in his commentary on Romans, C.E.B. Cranfield adopts the common interpretation that Paul is referring to a shift from the Sabbath to Sunday, reflecting the majority view regarding this passage, particularly in verses 5-6.[101] However, it cannot be clearly substantiated that Romans 14 is dealing with the Sabbath, primarily because the word Sabbath does not appear anywhere in the text. There are three plausible sources of the disagreement over "days" that Paul is referencing. The first, as mentioned earlier, is the dispute between the Pharisees and Sadducees regarding the counting of the Omer. The second could stem from differences over which days of the week were designated for fasting.[102] The third possibility is that the days related to pagan festivals, during which marketplace meats were likely products of pagan sacrifices.[103] Paul's emphasis

---

their taxes (*fiscus Judaicus*) and Jews should pay the tax as well (even though it is unjust). Rather, what Church history has shown is that in order to distance themselves from any association with Jewish rebels during the time of Hadrian, it became advantageous to have doctrines that showed no association, for any perceived association, whether the Sabbath or other Moedim, would have brought severe distress, much like that in the time of Nero.

100 "Let us then have nothing in common with the detestable Jewish crowd…all should unite in desiring that which sound reason appears to demand and in avoiding all participation in the perjured conduct of the Jews." Eusebius, *Life of Constantine*, 3.18-19. https://www.newadvent.org/fathers/25023.htm (Accessed April 2, 2024).

101 C.E.B. Cranfield, *Romans*, vol. 2, (T&T Clark, 1975), 705.

102 See, e.g., Lk. 18:12 and Didache 8:1; see also m. *Ta'anit* 2:4. Rabbinic sources prohibit fasting on Shabbat and other Festival days (the main exception is Yom Kippur, where "humble yourselves" is taken as a command for fasting. See Num. 29:8; Is. 58:6-14). b. *Eruvin* 41a; b. *Ta'anit* 10a.

103 This could connect Rom. 14 and 1 Cor. 8 & 10. Logan Williams and Paul T. Sloan,

that this matter is based on personal opinion (Rom. 14:1) suggests to the reader that the issue is halachic in nature, rather than involving a major doctrinal shift or altering the status of God's Word. However, it remains binding for those who choose to receive it. Given the status of dogma, the text cannot be referring to the Omer count as the source of the disagreement, and likewise, it makes the idea of moving the Sabbath an impossibility. It also cannot mean that Paul is allowing the consumption of unclean meats, as these matters are concretely settled in the Torah and are thus not based on personal opinion. In other words, it was understood that believers in Rome would be observing these commands. Such a transition would have been far more significant than a matter of personal opinion for Paul and for the congregants in Rome and beyond. Furthermore, if Paul taught the abolition of any of these commands in Romans 14, he would be committing apostasy from Moses, and the charges against him in Acts 21 would have been true. Considering the actual context found in Romans 14, reading Sabbath abolition into this passage is to commit eisegesis, inserting the theology of Sunday into the text, which is unwarranted by the text and anachronistic.

Regarding the supposed transition in Acts 20:7-12, first, the context shows a meeting that started in the evening and went late into the night "on the first day of the week." I ask why didn't they just meet Sunday morning like normal people who sleep during the night hours? Keener indicates that the presence of "many lamps" indicated that the

---

"Neither Sabbath nor Kashrut, but a Demonic Third Thing: Pagan Holidays and Food Sacrificed to Idols in Romans 14:1-23," (Paper presented at the 2023 Institute for Biblical Research Annual Conference, San Antonio, TX, November 2023).

people here in Troas were prepared for an extended "nocturnal teaching."[104] The text does not seem to be describing a regular gathering.

Second, there is nothing here that demonstrates a transition from the Sabbath as the official day of worship nor the day of commanded rest that was founded at the beginning of the world. John McArthur makes an indicative remark surrounding the Sabbath and Sunday: "Remember what I told you last time about the Sabbath Day? The Sabbath was the seventh day of the week...so, the New Covenant has its own day, a day in which we focus on God as our savior."[105] In fact, McArthur makes a similar appeal as this book to an earliest orthopraxy:

> "On the first day of the week, when we were gathered together to break bread"—isn't that interesting? No law has been given to establish this, but here we are well into the ministry of the Apostle Paul. Years have passed since the resurrection of Jesus Christ, and it's not remarkable, it's matter of fact...This church at Troas is exemplary of the Pattern of Sunday worship in the early church and ever since.[106]

Craig Keener, however, points out the problem with this view, underscoring that the narrative need not assume that this particular gathering in Troas was permanent.[107] Rather, the context in Acts emphasizes Paul's brief stopover. Keener says that this meeting could "point to a practice that was unusual; in any case, Paul met with the

---

104 Craig Keener, *Acts: An Exegetical Commentary*, vol. 3 (Baker Academic, 2014), 2970.

105 John McArthur, "Why Sunday is the Lord's Day," https://www.gty.org/library/sermons-library/90-380/~/about. (Accessed March 31, 2024). PDF transcript, 4, 12.

106 Ibid.

107 One should also note that Luke records in verses 5-6 that Paul and others were continuing to observe the Torah festivals.

believers at length then because he would leave soon afterward."[108] Furthermore, other texts that say the earliest believers were meeting daily and had daily activities associated with their ministry, so there is no real reason to *assume* that this text indicates a shift to Sunday worship.[109] The text makes no mention of worship; the exceptional circumstances of the meeting at Troas—Paul's imminent departure and the accidental death followed by a miraculous resurrection—mark this gathering as a unique event that Luke chose to record. Although this meeting could have been a regular meeting, there is no biblical evidence to support this being any replacement or transition away from the Sabbath. Interpreting the text as an abolition of the Sabbath imposes a second-century theological assumption of Sunday worship where it is not explicitly stated.[110]

An additional argument against the meeting at Troas representing a transition away from the Sabbath takes into account the widespread presence of slavery and the economic conditions of the time. It seems improbable that many Gentiles, whether enslaved or free, would have been allowed to take the Sabbath day off.[111] Instead, the slaves would

---

108 Craig Keener, *Acts*, 2962-2969.

109 See, e.g., Acts 6:1; 16:5; 17:11; 19:9; 2 Cor. 11:28.

110 C.K.A. Barrett, *Acts: A Critical and Exegetical Commentary on the Acts of the Apostles* (T&T Clark, 1994,1998), 951-52. Both Messianic and Adventist theologies underscore that the Scriptural evidence either decreeing or clearly delineating a transition from Sabbath to Sunday is severely lacking, and the transition only gains its momentum well into the second century and is also geographically centered in Rome or Alexandria. However, in Asia Minor, Palestine (as shown above), and even in places such as Ethiopia or further out in Asia, the persistence of Sabbath continued, being geographically separated from the influence of the bishops in Rome or Alexandria. See Heye, *Sabbath in Ethiopia: An Exploration of Christian Roots* (Center for Creative Ministry, 2003), 37-39, 48, 60.

111 Keener, *Acts*, 2966.

have had to finish their tasks before they could do anything else. Given this economic milieu, it is possible that whoever was leading the home fellowship at Troas may have held a gathering on the "first day of the week" to facilitate meeting for those unable to meet at the normal time at synagogue. If this had been a regular gathering, rather than the impromptu meeting discussed above, it appears that the leaders at Troas may have set aside time to "meet daily" to minister to believers. This gathering could have resembled a traditional Oneg feast or even a Bible study. In that, after the traditional Sabbath services, people gather together to break bread and to discuss the text and even do some teaching. Again, the context is especially relevant in 1 Cor. 11:33 where Paul instructs the congregation to wait on those who would be late to the Lord's Supper. Therefore, instead of showing a transition, the evening gatherings were not in replacement of the Sabbath, but are additions to assist those who could not attend the traditional Shabbat services, or for the collection of money (1 Cor. 16:1-3), or for ministering and "meeting daily" as was common by this time. Lastly, it seems that the apostles were taking the opportunity to continue teaching the Messianic connections to the weekly Parashah portions that were covered during the traditional service. These teachings happened after the traditional synagogue service and occurred from the evening to late at night. It would be like going to "Sunday night church" but occurring on Saturday night (which begins the first day of the week). Whatever the case may be, as Keener and others demonstrate, there is no contextual grounding to infer that the meeting in Acts 20:7 is indicative of a transition to a new understanding of the Sabbath, nor a replacement of the Sabbath.

Regarding the supposed transition in 1 Corinthians 16:1-3, which is the only other reference to believers gathering on "the first day of the week," the context appears to be in reference to the collection of money.

The text, like Acts 20:7, does not seem to present a command from Paul that abolishes or overrides the Sabbath, and there is no reason to interpret it as such. If there is any command, it simply commands the saving or storing up of money for those in Jerusalem. It is well known that handling money and collecting money on the Sabbath has always, traditionally, been viewed as inappropriate. The synagogues and the Temple use boxes for the collection of tithes and offerings instead of a direct handling of money (Lk. 21:1-2). The money is collected the next day, after sundown at the end of the Sabbath. In this text, the Apostles are simply collecting funds at the same time. Rather than abolishing the Sabbath, they could be maintaining a tradition regarding the handling of money, and there is no justification in the text for imposing a transition in worship.

Regarding the supposed transition in Colossians 2, the historical interpretation of this text that Paul regarded the Sabbath as either completely defunct or a matter of adiaphora, especially for Gentiles, goes back to at least Tertullian.[112] Many of the major names in Protestant theology interpret Colossians 2:8-17 in the same manner.[113] As Bacchiocchi writes:

> [Colossians 2:8-17] has been interpreted quite consistently to mean that Paul regarded the Sabbath as an Old Testament typological institution fulfilled by Christ and therefore no longer binding on Christians. Since this interpretation has

---

112 Tertullian, *Against Marcion* 5.19.

113 See Augustine, *Sermons on New Testament Lessons* 86.3. https://www.newadvent.org/fathers/160386.htm (Accessed May 2, 2024).; John Calvin, *Commentaries on the Epistle of Paul to the Philippians, Colossians, and Thessalonians*, trans. John Pringle (Christian Classics Ethereal Library). https://ccel.org/ccel/calvin/calcom42/calcom42.i.html (Accessed May 2, 2024). Bacchiocchi, *From Sabbath to Sunday*, 340.

been 'hallowed' by history, to submit the Colossians and related passages to a new critical scrutiny may appear as a pretentious undertaking. Yet this is a service that needs to be rendered to test the validity of any inherited interpretation.[114]

Whether there is a transition in Colossians 2 hinges on the historical context and what heresy or false teaching Paul is addressing. In other words, is Paul addressing the Law of God directly (as the majority of history has suggested) or is he speaking to something else?

Beginning in Colossians 2:8, one receives the first clue as to what Paul may be addressing, that being *the philosophy, human tradition, and elemental spirits* which resulted in both theological error and errors in orthopraxy (syncretism and asceticism).[115] The text suggests that this philosophy is man-made (*paradosis*; v. 2:8) and claims to offer wisdom (*sophia*; v. 2:3, 23), knowledge (*gnosis*; v. 2:2,3; 3:10), and understanding (*sunesis*; v. 1:9, 2:2) in a manner *not* "in accordance with Christ" (v. 8). In order to obtain this type of enlightenment, these Colossian "philosophers" were persuading the communities there to worship or venerate the angelic principalities and the elemental elements of the cosmos in order to have guaranteed access to the fullness of the divine (*pleroma*; v. 2:9-10; cf. 2:8, 10, 15, 18, 20). To that end, Arnold, Newsom, and others demonstrate a unique confluence of factors that is actually quite different than the other examples which have been

---

114 Bacchiocchi, *From Sabbath to Sunday*, 342.

115 Clinton E. Arnold, *The Colossian Syncretism: The Interface between Christianity and Folk Belief at Colossae* (Baker, 1996), 218. Arnold quotes Hippolytus regarding the teachings of Elchasai (see *A Refutation of all Heresies* 9.11) as an example of how Christianity was being infected locally by some form of syncretism either of Jewish Henotheism or Paganism.

touched on above (primarily Jewish oral law).[116] Instead of addressing Jewish oral halakha, Paul is confronting a unique sect, probably of Gentile origin, that has combined Phrygian folk religion, Jewish mystical angelology, the Law of God, and portions of apostolic teachings.[117] This sect, although likely accepting Christ, had been invoking either magical incantations to call upon or venerate angels, which ultimately caused a "diminution of one's relationship to Yahweh (and now Christ), in favor of a manipulative relationship with angels."[118]

The practices of this sect may have included forced circumcision (2:11), restrictions on certain foods and drinks (2:16, 21), a rigid and ascetic observance of sacred days, festivals, new moons, and the Sabbath (2:16), as well as harsh treatment of the body (2:23). These actions were likely aimed at achieving righteousness, protection from spiritual forces, or attaining enlightenment.[119] On the matter of cir-

---

116   Interestingly, Paul does not employ the word *nomos* (law) in this text, which seems to indicate that he is not making a distinction between the Law of God and the Oral Laws. This nuanced distinction will be addressed more thoroughly in the following chapter regarding the Conciliatory Theory, particularly 1 Corinthians 9.

117   On the Gentile origin of this sect, see G.B. Carid, *Paul's Letters From Prison* (Oxford University Press, 1976), 198; Bacchiocchi, *From Sabbath to Sunday*, 346 (Especially footnote 19); Arnold, *The Colossian Syncretism*, 91-102; 228-244; Carol Newsom, *Songs of the Sabbath Sacrifice: A Critical Edition*, Harvard Semitic Studies, vol. 27 (Brill, 1985), 16. On Jewish syncretic practice, see Philo, *Decalogue* 53. See also Jubilees 2:2; 1 QM 10.11-12. Of particular interest is the *Song of the Sabbath Sacrifice* (4QShirShabb), which has a significant emphasis on angelic veneration that demonstrates that within some sects of first-century Judaism this type of syncretic veneration was already taking place. Newsom points out that this type of worship was to "direct attention to the angels who praise rather than to the God who is praised."

118   Arnold, *The Colossian Syncretism*, 103.; See also, Bacchiocchi, *From Sabbath to Sunday*, 345.

119   Cha, *Galatians*, 120. Bacchiocchi notes that the severe treatment of the body is quite foreign to the philosophical assumptions within Judaism. In that, contra the more

cumcision, it has already been covered above, so there is no need to rehash the topic here.[120] On the matter of food and drink, it seems that the Greek here is pointing to the *act* of eating and drinking, not about delineating what is proper food or drink.[121] The philosophy had rules and regulations not only about what to eat (which could be considered biblical), but added to this extreme ascetic practice (2:23), including long fasting and starvation to please and receive protection from the powers and principalities.[122] As for the new moons, festivals, and Sabbaths, O'Brien notes that the moedim, given by God through his Law, were one of the primary indicators of Israel's election.[123] However, here at Colossae these Holy Days were mixed with other religious ideas and practices that were foreign to the Torah and the God of Israel.[124] In this respect, the observance of these days in connection with these gods or angels is decidedly *against* what the written Torah commands.

However, what exactly was nailed to the cross? (Col 2:14) Interestingly, Paul does not use the term *nomos* ("law") to refer to what was

---

dualist ascetics which were more common in Greek philosophy and also subsequently in Alexandrian Christianity (think Origen and his own mutilation), Judaism of the first century was against such abasement. See Bacchiocchi, *From Sabbath to Sunday*, 354-354.

120 See also Benjamin Szumskyj, "The Role of the Law in the Sanctification of the Believer Today: A Brief Introduction to Pronomianism," Ph.D Dissertation (Liberty University, 2024), 142.

121 Βρῶσις and πόσις (eating and drinking). See Johannes Behm, *TDNT* (Grand Rapids, MI: Eerdmans, 1968), vol. I, 642 and Leonhard Goppelt, *TDNT* VI, 145-148. Given that Moses is silent on beverages also seems to indicate that Paul is not speaking about the Law of God but the philosophy in question.

122 Arnold, *The Colossian Syncretism*, 311; Wilber, *Remember the Sabbath*, 58-59.

123 Peter T. O'Brien, *Word Biblical Commentary: Colossians, Philemon* (Thomas Nelson, 1982), 139.

124 Douglas Moo, *Pillar New Testament Commentary: The Letter to the Colossians and to Philemon* (Eerdmans, 2008), 221.

nailed to the cross. Rather, he develops his argument through a "certificate of debt consisting of decrees against us, which was hostile to us." Rightfully, the Torah does demand the death penalty for some sins, primarily sins like apostasy and idolatry. However, a relevant question that presents itself is how would abolishing the commandments of God provide any real assurance of forgiveness? Simply removing the law does not provide forgiveness for anything, it simply removes potential future guilt from sin because, technically, there would not be any sin—if there were no legal decrees against us from the time of the cross, there is nothing that needs to be satisfied. Rather, given the absence of the term *nomos*, it seems that it is not the law as the standard that is nailed to the cross, but rather our violation and guilt according to that law. It is our record of transgressions against that law which is nailed to the cross (cf. 1 Jn. 3:4). In other words, God destroyed the written record of our sins and not the *legal grounding* of sin. Furthermore, it seems that without a law, there would actually be no such thing as mercy. Bacchiocchi makes an astute connection regarding the mercy of God and the written record of our sins in that "By destroying the evidence of our sins God has also 'disarmed the principalities and powers' (2:15), since it is no longer possible for them to function as the accusers of the brethren (Rev. 12:10)."[125] So, in this regard, the heresy at Colossae is doubly wrong for trying to please divine powers to garner favor, when the record of debt was truly forgiven by God through the Messiah. The ascetics of this philosophy, in their feelings of inadequacy, were, through punishment of the body, attempting to bring about forgiveness and protection in a continuous cycle of debt payments to these angelic powers. Paul's argument is that

---

125 Bacchiocchi, *From Sabbath to Sunday*, 351.

these divine beings need not concern you, as your record of debt has already been paid.

But what does Paul mean when he says that the practices mentioned in Colossians 2:16 are a "shadow of things to come"? Having seen what the philosophy at Colossae was teaching and its practical outworking, Paul's teaching in verse 17 can now be analyzed. Although it is commonly interpreted that Christ rendered all the Holy Days of the Torah unimportant, I believe the historical context and syncretism in Colossae suggest that Paul's reference to "shadows" serves as a powerful lesson, rather than indicating a transition away from the Torah. To begin it should be without question that everything in the word of God (the Scriptures) is a written and derivative form of the person of God, and as such can only point us to the very concrete person of God.[126] Interestingly, to this point, Paul says that these feasts are shadows of "things to come," and therefore, *not* things that have already transpired. Paul is seemingly looking toward a future fulfillment of these days, with all of them having been, and continuing to be, centered on Christ. Wilber writes, "These commands function not only in memorializing Yeshua's work of atonement on the cross but also continue to point forward to his future work to occur at the end of the age."[127] Given this, like all ceremonial rites and celebrations, they inherently point to a greater reality.[128] At Colossae, unfortunately, the philoso-

---

126 Morrison, *Has God Said?*, loc. 209 (Kindle).

127 Wilber, *Remember the Sabbath*, 60-61.

128 For example, are not fireworks on the American Independence Day (July 4) symbolic of the "Star Spangled Banner" (bombs bursting in air), which itself is representative of the Battle of Ft. McHenry during the War of 1812, which was essentially the second war for American Independence? In other words, all celebrations and memorials always point to a larger narrative. The derivative shadows of the Torah are the same. They point to the single greatest reality, that being the Creator and Master of the universe.

phy had used these days and ascetic practices to venerate and appease other and inferior angelic/demonic beings. But the signposts of the Torah should be used for worshipping the Messiah, for this is what the Moedim point to. Paul, therefore, is not condemning or transitioning away from the Torah; rather, he is correcting an errant sect of syncretic Judaism that began to misappropriate the shadows through man-made philosophy. To that end, shadows are not unimportant—far from it! They are the ever-present and God-breathed reminder of the light, for shadows do not exist unless the light first exists.[129] Since Christ was raised from the dead and had yet to return, Paul's emphasis on "the things to come" confirms that the shadows are the current reality of God's promises to redeem both Jew and Gentile.[130] Instead of using "shadow" as a pejorative, as the transitory theory and others since Tertullian would proclaim, Paul's use seems to be more indicative of viewing the shadows as a majestic reminder of past, present, and future redemption, thus necessitating their continued importance in the life of believers.

In closing, it seems that the contexts of the above passages do not support the notion of the Sabbath transitioning. Furthermore, given the preponderance of indications of direct commands to keep the Sabbath and no specific command or prophesy to abolish the Sabbath, and Paul's indication to James that he did not apostatize from Moses, the above passages should be read in a way that upholds the Law as opposed to transitioning the Law, abolishing the Law, or replacing the

---

129 Ps. 119:105 says, "Your word is a lamp to my feet and a light to my path." Jesus says in Jn. 9:5, "I am the light of the world." The derivative light will always be dimmer than the source and substance of the light.

130 It has not happened yet (because heaven and earth have not passed away). Paul says in 1 Cor. 13:12 that "For *now* we see in a mirror dimly, but *then* face to face; *now* I know in part, but *then* I will know fully just as I also have been fully known" (Italics added).

Law with new dogma. If the apostles created new Dogma that transitioned the Sabbath to "the first day of the Week" they would actually be guilty of Christ's rebuke of the Pharisees in Mark 7. Through their traditions, they would be making void the Law of God and the Sabbath, which has remained on the seventh day since the beginning of time.

Historical Context and Different Rules For Gentiles

Acts 21:19 shows that myriads were coming to faith, many of whom were Gentiles. These new Gentile converts, having been mostly steeped in pagan religion and culture, were completely unfamiliar with the standard of holy conduct (cf. Eph. 2:12)[131] Before coming to faith, these Gentiles were participating in pagan rituals (at least at a level of cultural participation), which included all sorts of unclean practices, fornication, strangulation, drinking blood, among a myriad of other sins. All of these things are prohibited by the Torah or are against the spirit of the Torah. The question that should be asked in regard to the context presented to the reader is, could any new Gentile believer continue to practice these things while in fellowship with people who follow the Law of Moses? The obvious answer is no. Furthermore, what is quite interesting is that these Gentiles have no idea what the Law of God fully contains. When someone gets saved, even today, do they know everything? Of course not. New believers must start somewhere. What the apostles determined to show is that the first step for covenant inclusion is not circumcision; rather, it was faith. Therefore, knowing that they are saved by grace through faith

---

131   Ben Witherington III, *The Acts of the Apostles* (Eerdmans, 1998), 463; Matthew Thiessen, *Contesting Conversion* (Oxford University Press, 2011), 148; C.G. Montegiore and H.M.J Loewe, eds., *A Rabbinic Anthology*), 570; m. *Horayot* 3:8; m. *Bikkurim* 1:4.

and not by proselyte circumcision (which is Pharisaical dogma), they are allowed entry into the community (the Politeia of Israel) because they have attached themselves to the Most High through Messiah and have agreed to walk in his ways. An astute reader would note that this is indeed similar to the Israelites at Mt. Sinai (Ex. 19). The people agreed to do all that the LORD says before they even received the Law (Ex. 19:8). The Israelites were saved out of Egypt and then received the Torah. . Likewise, when someone is brought from darkness to light (Acts 26:18), though their knowledge is incomplete, they affirm that they *will obey what they do not yet fully know.* Here, the Gentiles are commanded to immediately stop all pagan worship practices and to act and behave as Abraham did (cf. Jn. 8:39).

These dogmata are said to be good to the Holy Spirit (Acts 15:28). Why is this? Well, because it is the Holy Spirit's role to write the Torah on their heart as promised in the New Covenant (Jer. 31:31-33). The Holy Spirit is in the business of sanctification, which indicates that the Gentiles were to grow into obedience, hence the expectation found in Acts 15:21.[132] Again, there is no reason to have Moses preached to Gentiles if the Law was abolished.[133] These dogmata for the Gentiles

---

132 In his article, "Acts 15:21: Moses is Preached and Read in the Synagogues," *JETS* 65.4 (2022), 707-717, Charles Savelle lays out five differing interpretations of this passage. The first view is that "Jewish teachings and practices are unaffected." The second, "The decrees are consistent with the teaching of Torah concerning Gentiles." The third, "The view that Gentiles can still learn Torah." The fourth, "The view regarding the historical effect of synagogue proclamation upon Gentiles." The fifth, "The view that Jewish sensibilities are a rational for the decree." Savelle also concedes that interpreters can also intermix these options choosing to combine the various explanations (p.717). Accordingly, I, much like Polhill, view that several of the options are at play, primarily options 1, 2, 3, 5. See John B. Polhill, *Acts*, vol. 26, The New American Commentary (Nashville, TN: Broadman & Holman, 1992), 331-332.

133 G.K. Chesterton, "Enemies of Property" in *G.K. Chesterton Collected Works: Family,*

are thus practical and immediate requirements for entrance into the community, not the total body of rules and regulations by which they should love, which is only found in the Tanakh and the teachings of the apostles.

Acts 15:28 gives another clue in that the Gentiles were not to be burdened with more dogmata than these *essentials* at the beginning of their journey. The Greek word used for "essentials" is *epanagkes*. This word carries with it the meaning of "necessarily required"—in fact, so necessary that they can be compelled.[134] The rest of the Law would be learned from Sabbath to Sabbath. Thus, the apostles will not compel (by force) the Gentiles to follow the Law of Moses (or the rabbinic halacha). Rather, it is the job of the Holy Spirit to *impel* them to obedience, as the Law, interpreted and lived out by Messiah, is being written on their hearts.[135] However, the new Gentile converts need an essential and objective starting point, guided by *the apostles* (as opposed to the yoke of the Pharisees or other sects), not only to give assurance to the existing members of the congregation of the Gentiles' obedience and commitment to the God of Israel, but also demonstrate saving faith.

What can be determined from all this? First, in order to even have fellowship with the apostles (who are Jews) and the Jews in general, the new Gentile converts must adhere to some minimum essentials: faith in the Messiah and no pagan rituals.[136] They would willingly obey, be compelled to obey, or else be kicked out. Second, entry requirements are not based on the status of the flesh, nor of ethnicity. All Jews and

---

Society, Politics, vols. IV (Ignatius Press, 1987), 64.

134 Thayer's, G1876.

135 *Ennomos Christos*. 1 Cor. 9.

136 Gentiles are grafed into an existing structure.

Greeks are justified by faith. But a pivotal verse highlights the necessity of sanctification, rooted in a clear and written standard. It cannot be overstated: there is a distinct difference between justification and the sanctification mandated by Scripture. Hence, Acts 15:21 raises a truly startling question: if there was an evolutionary transition away from Moses, and the Gentiles only had four rules to keep in perpetuity, then why expose them to Moses every Sabbath where he is preached? The answer is, if the apostles were transitioning away from the Law, there would be absolutely no reason to expose the Gentiles to the Law. On these grounds, the transitory theory does not conform to the reality of the biblical text. By contrast, the reason the Gentiles should hear Moses preached becomes much clearer when considering their sanctification: they would learn the righteous requirements of the Law every Sabbath and would conform themselves to it, through the work of the Holy Spirit. In short, they would learn the truth by doing the truth (cf. Ps. 119:142). They would walk according to the perfect Law of liberty (Ps. 119:45; Jas. 1:25). They would walk *ennomos Christos*.

This personal transformation and sanctification, therefore, represent a *true and biblical* transitory theory: the Gentile believers would develop into men and women of God, moving into the fullness of God. The real transition is transformation. Thus, the four laws of Acts 15 were only entry requirements, a first-century version of a seeker-friendly ekklesia.

Concluding the Transitory Theory

In this chapter, I have sought to demonstrate that the biblical text does not present a transition or the creation of a new religion for Gentiles. I have shown that the transitory theory fails philosophically and hermeneutically and does not correspond to the historical reality presented in Scripture. It is my contention that the only transition presented in the scriptures is a transition away from theological error, back toward the preexisting standard, which is the Law of God, written by the hand of Moses, lived out by the Messiah, and upheld by the apostles, the foremost being Paul. Since Paul insisted he did not apostatize/transition away from Moses, then the most logical solution is that the Pauline epistles should not be read via the Transitory Theory.

CHAPTER 3

CONCILIATION AND APPEASEMENT

Having dealt with the transitory theory, with its penchant for evolutionary theology and its inability to ground itself in the earliest historical and biblically-based sources, the primary hurdle remaining for the Continuous Theory is to reconcile with the idea of being "all things to all men." This concept, based on 1 Corinthians 9:22, serves as a cornerstone for the Conciliatory Theory. In order to explain the actions of Paul and James in Acts 21, the Conciliatory Theory posits that Paul and James are making a conciliatory action toward the Jews, who are apparently *overzealous* for the Law. A quote from the NET Bible translator notes illustrates this theory in no uncertain terms:

> That is, undergo ritual cleansing. Paul's cleansing would be necessary because of his travels in 'unclean' Gentile territory. This act would represent a conciliation gesture. Paul would have supported a 'law-free' mission to the Gentiles as an option, but this gesture would represent an attempt to be sensitive to the Jews (1 Cor. 9:15-22).[1]

Polhill also presents another version of the conciliatory theory that revolves around historical compromise, but also rests on similar assumptions as the interpretative note found in the NET:

---

1   Note Acts 21:24, "ae," *NET Bible*, 2nd ed. (Biblical Studies Press, 2017), 2109.

The elders' proposal (vv. 22–24) was strictly for Paul, that he as a Jewish Christian demonstrate his fidelity to the law to offset the rumors in the Jewish Christian community. *It was a sort of compromise solution and thoroughly in accord with the picture of James at the Jerusalem Conference.* The apostolic decrees were themselves a type of compromise. James wanted both to acknowledge the legitimacy of Paul's law-free Gentile mission and to maintain an effective witness among the Jews, for which faithfulness to the law was absolutely essential. Ultimately the *compromise* did not work—either in this instance for Paul or in regard to the larger issue of the relationship between Jewish and Gentile Christianity... As Jewish nationalism increased, the Gentile mission became more and more of a liability to Jewish Christianity. In the aftermath of the Jewish War with Rome and the fall of Jerusalem in a.d. 70, Jewish Christianity was declared heretical by official Judaism; and it was no longer possible for a Christian Jew to remain in the Jewish community. James had seen the problem well and sought to present himself as a strict, Torah-abiding Jew, doubtless to strengthen the credibility of his witness to his fellow Jews. Ultimately, he gave his life for his Christian witness, being put to death at the order of the high priest Ananus in a.d. 62.[2]

---

2   John B. Polhill, *Acts: An Exegetical and Theological Exposition of Holy Scripture*, vol. 26, The New American Commentary (Broadman & Holman Publishers, 1992), 449–450. As shown above from the historical analysis conducted within the section on the Transitory Theory regarding the change from Sabbath to Sunday, Polhill, likewise, does an excellent job at showing historical influences for the division of the early synagogue and the Christians. Likewise, adding to Pohill's analysis, Bacchiocchi shows that there were also significant Pagan and civil/social pressures that the believing gentiles and Jews

The theories presented here have at least one major problem, some major assumptions, and a few misinterpretations that need to be addressed.

"Unclean" Gentile Territory—The Major Historical and Scriptural Problem

The founding axiom of the Conciliatory theory is that Gentiles and Gentile territory were considered unclean.[3] As previously discussed, certain groups within Judaism did indeed exhibit hostility toward Gentiles, even after their proselyte conversion, viewing Gentile-dominated areas as sources of contamination. There is also evidence suggesting that some Jews would undergo ritual baths after being in predominantly *Jewish* areas.[4] However, the primary historical

---

both believing and unbelieving would have felt as well, especially in the diaspora. The Jesus Movement of this time was the target of both Pagan milieu and hostility from unbelieving Jews. As for Polhill's conjecture about whether or not James was shrewd enough to foresee this increase of unbelieving Jewish nationalism, and thus attempt to show his loyalty to the Torah leaves a little to be desired, as then obedience to Torah by this point in history is for mere prudential self-interest, as opposed to a heartfelt devotion and obedience to the Messiah. In the biblical narrative, it is the obedience to the Torah which serves as the means by which the Prophets are condemned. As in, those commissioned by God in all the biblical narrative call the people back to the Torah and are punished and killed. In essence, Torah following is either met by gentile hostility and/ or hostility from apostate Israel. However, Polhill and others seemingly flip the script and want to have Torah obedience be the means of self-preservation for the apostles. As in, they feared for their lives, even though they knew it was either wrong or unneeded. See also David A. DeSilva, *Honor, Patronage, Kinship, and Purity: Unlocking New Testament Culture* (IVP, 2022), 137-184.

3   See *Ketubot* 110b; *Avodah Zerah* 8a.

4   Matthew Thiessen, *Contesting Conversion* (Oxford University Press, 2011), 148; C.G. Montegiore and H.M.J Loewe, eds., *A Rabbinic Anthology*), 570.; m. *Horayot* 3:8; m. *Bikkurim* 1:4.

problem is that the solution for such uncleanness, if it even existed, would have been a mikveh, not a vow—and definitely not a Nazirite vow, which appears to be the ceremony James suggests as the remedy.[5]

Now, besides this major flaw, what is actually more important scripturally is how the *apostles* viewed Gentiles by the time of the Second Jerusalem Council. In order to ascertain the apostles' view of Gentiles and what it means for the interpretation of Acts 21, one must first turn to Peter's vision in Acts 10 and 11 and Paul's rebuke of Peter in Galatians 2.

Peter's Vision—Acts 10-11 and Galatians 2

Acts 10 and 11 are often cited by interpreters to show that all "foods" are now clean to eat. They cite Peter's vision with all the animals, clean and unclean, coming down. The Lord says to Peter, "kill and eat" (Acts 10:13; 11:7). Peter then replies, "Not so Lord, I have never eaten anything common or unclean."[6] The voice of the Lord responds, "What God has cleansed, no longer consider unholy." Most have interpreted this text to be a slam-dunk case for the consumption of swine or other unclean meats.[7] The problem for the majority inter-

---

5   D.G. Dunn, *The Acts of the Apostles*, Narrative Commentary (Trinity Press International, 1996) 246-47; Luke Timothy Johnson, *The Acts of the Apostles*, ed. Daniel J. Harrington (Liturgical Press, 1992), 330; Ben Witherington III, *The Acts of the Apostles: A Socio-Rhetorical Commentary* (Wm. B. Eerdmans Publishing Co., 1998), 649-651.; Keener, *Acts*, vol. 3, 635-6.

6   This test of Peter's is actually very similar to that of the prophet Ezekiel. In Ez. 4:12, the Lord says to Ezekiel, "You shall eat it as a barley cake having baked it in their sight, over human dung." Ezekiel says in 4:14, "Ah, Lord GOD! Behold I have never been defiled; for from my youth until now I have never eaten what died of itself or was torn by beast, nor has any unclean meat ever entered my mouth" (e.g., nothing common or unclean). Two visions, two prophets, with essentially the same answer.

7   Fruchtenbaum, *Israelology* 890.; Ryrie says, "Nobody ever criticizes the dispensationalist

pretation is that Peter received an explicit interpretation of his vision. As Warfield points out, whenever a prophet is given a vision, it is always accompanied by an interpretation![8] First, Peter is greatly perplexed (Acts 10:17). This raises the question: if Christ declared all foods clean in Mark 7:19, why would Peter be confused here? It is my contention that Christ did not give permission for ham sandwiches or shrimp po'boys. In other words, if Christ taught the abolition of Leviticus 11, Peter would not be confused here, for Christ's teachings would have already been known, and a transition from Leviticus 11 would have already been established.[9] Furthermore, should one continue reading, Acts 10:28 gives the actual meaning of the vision: "God has shown me that I should not call any *man* unholy or unclean" (emphasis added). From this the reader can deduce that the whole context of Acts 10 and 11 was never about food at all! The context is about interaction between Jew and Greek. The point is that since the command to eat unclean meats is unlawful, Peter is searching for an alternative meaning to the vision. The interpretation comes when he is visited by the Gentiles who were sent by God. Peter says, "You yourselves know how unlawful it is for a man who is a Jew to associate

---

for teaching that the dietary regulation of the Mosaic Law have no application to the Christian." Charles Ryrie, *Dispensationalism* (Moody, 2007), 83; C.I. Schofield, *Scofield Reference Bible* (Oxford University Press, 1909), 94-95; Bahnsen states, about Acts 10, "the dream which taught him that no longer is any meat unclean." See *Theonomy*, 225-226. This interpretation is the majority view in both Reformed and Dispensational camps with very few exceptions like Rushdoony. See Rousas John Rushdoony, *Leviticus*, vol.3 of *Commentaries on the Pentateuch* (Ross House Books, 2005), 107-126.

8   Benjamin B. Warfield, *The Inspiration and Authority of the Bible*, ed. Samuel G. Craig (The Presbyterian and Reformed Publishing Company, 1948), 83-96.

9   Rabbi Shmuley Boteach, *Kosher Jesus* (Gefen Publishing House, 2012), 33, 124-125; Michael L. Brown, *The Real Kosher Jesus* (Charisma Media, 2012), 91-124.

with a foreigner or to visit him; and yet God has shown me that I should not call any man common or unclean."

Where is it written that it is unlawful to eat with Gentiles? During the first century, it seems to have been common practice to assume that all Gentiles were perpetually unclean due to their continued exposure to idolatry. This is evidenced by several rulings from Hillel, Shammai, and the writings of Josephus.[10] Biblically, this is confirmed to have been common place given Peter's and Barnabas's susceptibility and hypocrisy (cf. Gal 2). I invite everyone to examine the Tanakh for such a command, as the opposite is often found. For instance, Numbers 15:16 provides a clear example of Gentile inclusion, and the prophets also speak of all nations coming to Zion and the Temple being a house of prayer for all peoples (Is. 56:7; 66:23). As Hegg points out, instead of enmity between Israel and Gentiles, the Tanakh presents a totally different picture:

> The foreigner who desired to worship the God of Abraham,
> Isaac, and Jacob was to be welcomed into the community
> and treated with the same respect as we give the native born

---

10 Hillel and Shammai seem to have differing degrees of the impurity that Jews would incur should they come in contact with Gentiles: "A proselyte who converted on the eve of Passover – the House of Shammai say, 'He immerses and eats his Passover offering in the evening.' And the House of Hillel say, 'He who separates himself from his uncircumcision is as if he separated himself from the grave [and must be sprinkled on the third and seventh day after circumcision as if he had suffered corpse uncleanness].'" m. *Pesachim* 8:8. Here it becomes clear that Shammai thought the impurity was light. Josephus likewise records the stringent regime of the Essens in regard to foreigners saying, "Now after the time of their preparatory trial is over, they are parted into four classes; and so far are the juniors inferior to the seniors, that if the seniors should be touched by the juniors, they must wash themselves, as if they had intermixed themselves with the company of a foreigner." See *Wars of the Jews* 2.8.10.

(Ex. 22:21; 23:9; Lev. 19:33, 34, 25:35; Deut. 26:12). They were to be given full participation in matter of Torah and Torah-life (Sabbath, Ex. 23:12. cp. Is. 56:3ff; Gleanings, Lev. 19:19; Justice, Ex. 12:49; Lev. 24:22; Festivals, Deut. 16:11, 14; Worship and prayer in the temple, 1 Ki. 8:41-43; cp. 2 Chron. 6:32, 33). And the prophets pronounce judgment upon any who would neglect their God-given responsibilities to the 'stranger,' on the same grounds as neglect of orphans and widows (Ps. 94:6; Is. 56:3ff; Jer. 22:3; Zech. 7:10).[11]

Since one would search in vain to find such a law that separates Jewish and Gentile believers, the law that Peter must be speaking about is, again, the oral traditions and law (dogma) put in place by the rabbis, which violates the very intent of Israel to be a light unto the nations (Is. 42:6; 49:6). One cannot be a light to others if associating with different races results in automatic uncleanness. This dogmatic "unlawfulness" was, in itself, an unlawful yoke imposed by Jewish leadership, creating a dividing wall and fence around the actual Torah. These burdensome yokes and manmade commandments are the very "laws" Christ castigates in Mark 7:8, 10-13.

The Dividing Wall: An Excursus

The dogmatic dividing walls spoken about by Peter are also mentioned by Paul in Ephesians 2:14, wherein Christ destroyed (*katargeo*) the barrier (*phragmos*) of the dividing wall (*mesotoichos*), which is the law (*nomos*) of commandments (*entole*) in ordinances (*dogma*). At first glance, it might seem that Paul is referring to the Mosaic Law.

---

11 Tim Hegg, "Can we Speak of 'Law" in the New Testament in Monolithic Terms?" Presented at *Evangelical Theological Society*, Northwest Region meeting (April 1995), 18.

However, it is important to note that the Law of Moses is never referred to as dogma in the Septuagint or the apostolic writings.[12] Dogma is only used in reference *man-made* ordinances or traditions. Thus, it seems what Paul is speaking about here is that it was the rabbis who were building unnecessary "fences" that were causing the enmity between Jew and Gentile.[13] It was the unwarranted traditions and continued denigration of Gentile converts that was creating enmity, not the perfect Law of God. Commandments that bar association between Jew and Greek are not found in the actual Torah of God and go against the crux of the Abrahamic covenant to bless all the nations of the earth. How can one be blessed if one is not even allowed to associate with the people of God because of a dogmatic wall of division? In fact, throughout his life, the Messiah clearly opposed the trend of separation prevalent in first-century Judaism, which sought to build dogmatic walls between different races. Instead, he aimed to reach out as a light, guiding people into alignment with the Word of God through repentance. Christ's actions are indicative of bucking against theological dogma to actually fulfill the will of God by the Word of God.

Although it is true that Josephus uses the phrase *ho mesos toixos* "the middle wall" to describe the physical wall preventing Gentile and unclean Jewish visitors to the temple from proceeding into the court of the Jews, it is never described or designated as *phragmos* by Josephus or in any other ancient writings.[14] In fact, the physical wall itself was

---

12 In 3 Maccabees 1:3, dogmaton can rightfully be translated as traditions or ancestral traditions. See Bruce Metzger, *Oxford Annotated Apocrypha: Apocrypha of the Old Testament* (Oxford University Press, 1977), 295.

13 *Pirkei Avot* 1.1.

14 Josephus, *Antiquities* 8.3-4. https://www.gutenberg.org/files/2848/2848-h/2848-h.htm#link8noteref-12 (accessed August 8, 2023). As for the legal authority to build such

inscribed with the word *drufaktou* and the warning not to proceed. Paul would have been well aware of the physical, unlawful wall at the Temple, so it seems likely that he would have used its common name, *drufaktou*, if he were referring to the physical wall.[15] That being said, the physical barrier at the temple is merely the concrete representation of the dogma.[16] Accordingly, the Greek grammar, as Cha argues, is that the genitive be understood appositionally. Thus, *to mesotoixon tou phragmos* should be understood as "the barrier consisting of the fence," which refers to the dogmatic ordinances that brought separation between Jew and Gentile.[17] The physical wall and the theological separation are integrally connected, but dogma is a much harder barrier to resolve, as concrete walls can simply be knocked down, while ideas are a bit more pernicious.[18]

By imposing a physical barrier at the temple, creating doctrinal dogmatic divisions, and perpetuating racism, the Jews had violated the command to be a light to the nations. Therefore, it is highly likely that it is the dogmatic and social barriers which are the emphasis of

---

a wall, it is only found in tradition and nowhere in the Scriptures. As it is supposed to be a house of prayer for all nations. See Is. 2:2; Is 56:6-7; Is 66:20-23; Jer. 3:17.

15   Tim Hegg, *A Commentary on the Epistle to the Ephesians* (Torah Resource, 2019), 144.

16   Harold W. Hoehner, *Ephesians: An Exegetical Commentary* (Baker Academic, 2002), 59, 375-6.

17   M.I. Cha, *Misunderstanding Galatians: An Exegetical, Originalist Commentary* (Wipf and Stock, 2021), 18.

18   See m. *Avot* 1.1; The Epistle of Aristeas, which is dated 250-100BCE, is an early source that uses the word *phragmos* as a descriptor of the oral torah and as the dogmatic/halachic fence that separates the Jews from the Gentiles. R.H. Charles, ed., "The Letter of Aristeas," (The Clarendon Press, 1913), https://www.ccel.org/c/charles/otpseudepig/aristeas.htm (date accessed March 15, 2023).; See E.P. Sanders, *Judaism: Practice & Belief 63BCE-66CE* (Trinity Press International, 1992), 61.; Adolf Deissmann, *Light from the Ancient East* (Baker, 1978), 80.

Paul in the context of Ephesians 2:14-15. Paul is underscoring that Christ is the fullness of the Abrahamic covenant, by the making of one new man, and by ingrafting the Gentiles into the politeia of Israel. To that end, the dividing wall was not the Law of Moses, but rather refers to the unlawful dogma and those man-made regulations that go against the Word of God (cf. Mk. 7:6-13).

What about Peter's backsliding and Paul's rebuke in Galatians 2? Again, it is of utmost importance to remember the chronological order of the text: (1) Peter's vision, (2) Paul's mission to Galatia and the penning of Galatians, and (3) The actions recorded in Acts 21. Peter, having already had the vision in Acts 10, begins acting hypocritically by refusing to eat with Gentiles, so Paul rebukes him in Galatians 2 because he is reconstructing the dividing wall! What this means historically is that James and Paul affirm that Gentiles are "clean" according to Peter's earlier vision and the explicit instruction of the Lord. It is Peter who is not following the correct doctrine, which is why he stands condemned by Paul in Galatians 2.

The Failure of the Idea of "Unclean Gentile Territory" in the Conciliatory Theory

In Acts 21, we encounter Paul and James following both Peter's vision and Paul's earlier rebuke of Peter in Galatians. If, as the Conciliatory Theory contends, Paul was required to purify himself after his travels in "unclean Gentile territory" simply to appease the Jews that were "zealous for the Law," then both Paul and James would be just as guilty of hypocrisy as Peter was in Galatians. Considering that both James and Paul understood that Gentiles were declared clean by God (recognizing that Gentiles were never inherently unclean but that faulty theology within first-century Judaism was being corrected), and that there is no law in the written Torah suggesting that Gentiles are ontologically unclean, nor does the Torah state that Gentiles are irrevocably defiled (*koinoo*) by their idols, it is impossible that the apostles would affirm a cleansing ceremony for Paul solely due to the fact that he was in a Gentile-dominated area. Doing so would make James and Paul guilty of the same error as Peter, and even worse, it would establish this as doctrine through the Second Jerusalem Council, directly contradicting the revelation given to Peter in Acts 10.

The notion of unclean Gentiles in the Conciliatory Theory is not only untenable as doctrine—making Paul, James, and Peter all hypocrites—but it is also utterly unbiblical. This conclusion is based on a proper interpretation of both the Abrahamic covenant (which promises that all the nations of the earth will be blessed) and the consistent, cohesive, and comprehensive understanding of Peter's vision. Lastly and importantly, confirming the analysis above, is that the purification that Paul undergoes is likely for the Nazirite Vow. What is interesting is that the other four people under a vow purify themselves, too! The context makes it seem that these four men were in Jerusalem with James and not with Paul in Gentile territory, so why should they need purification if they were not in Gentile territory? This obviously means that the purification was not for travel (because contextually the other four were with James in supposedly clean territory), but the purification is for the *legal requirements* of the vow to prove Paul's innocence against the charge of apostasy. The only logical conclusion, then, is that Paul undertakes this purification ritual in order to perform the Nazirite Vow (thus proving he has not committed apostasy) and not to cleanse himself after travelling amongst the Gentiles (whom Paul already considers clean) based on his earlier rebuke of Peter! Thus, historically, contextually, and hermeneutically, the assertions of the Conciliatory Theory fail.

But What About "All Things to All Men?"

Although the Conciliatory Theory is on dangerously thin ice, as demonstrated above, there may be a potential hermeneutical lifeline in 1 Corinthians 9:19-23. Here, Paul's actions could be seen as his effort to be "all things to all men." This, as pointed out by the translators note above, is the true crux of the Conciliatory Theory. Given what has been covered so far, how can one interpret Paul's words in Corinthians? Is there a "law-free" option as the Conciliatory/Appeasement/Compromise Theory contends? Are orthodoxy and orthopraxy culturally relative, even though elsewhere Jew and Gentiles are not separated (Eph. 2:11-12, Rom. 10:12; Rom. 11; Col. 3:11)? Surely, there is a way to synthesize mutually-exclusive truth claims without making Paul, James, and Peter hypocritical doctrinal chameleons.

> For though I am free from all men, I have made myself a slave to all, so that I may win more. To the Jews, I became as a Jew, so that I might win Jews; to those who are under the Law, as under the Law, though not being myself under the Law, so that I might win those who are under the Law; to those who are without law, as without law, though not being without the law of God, but under the law of Christ, so that I might win those who are without law. To the weak I became weak, that I might win the weak; I have become all things to all men, so that I may by all means save some. I do all things for the sake of the gospel, so that I may become a fellow partaker of it.
> —1 Corinthians 9:19-23

This passage occurs within the greater context of Paul's work at Corinth. Firstly, at Corinth, there were significant internal divisions that had happened, namely a conflict between those who follow Paul,

Apollos, and Cephas (1:32; 3:22). Secondly, these divisions were monumentally exacerbated by the acceptance of significant sexual sin (Ch. 5). Thirdly, the division had become so severe that members of the community found it necessary to pursue lawsuits in the pagan courts. These pagan court proceedings would have, in all likelihood, required a pagan sacrifice, which is an obvious violation of the dogmatic regulations from the First Jerusalem council (not to mention the prohibition against idolatry in the Torah itself). Fourthly, there were those within this synagogue who were members of the Party of the Circumcision, who believed that Gentiles must be circumcised in order to be saved. Fifthly, there were Jews who did not believe in Messiah. In short, Corinth was a doctrinal and pastoral nightmare.

Knowing this, the immediate textual context of ch. 8-10 is Paul's appeal to forfeit one's freedoms, if necessary, for the sake of the ones who are "weak." In 9:14-18, Paul shows that he gave up his right to be paid for his services so that he would be more effective in ministry. In fact, he describes himself as a slave (*doulos*), effectively relinquishing all personal rights.[19] This brings one to the text at hand, which begins with "for," which means one must ask, "What is that conjunction there for?" This conjunction connects verses 1-18 to verses 19-23. Thus, Paul's own example of forfeiting pay is directly linked to the example he is about to make. In other words, the reader should be viewing his passage within the context of the *relinquishing of personal freedom*, not the expansion of doctrinal freedom or allowing apostasy from Moses.

---

19 Yosef Koelner and Jeffrey Seif, *Sha'ul/Paul God's Shaliach (Apostle) Corresponds with the Corinthians* (Messianic Jewish Publishers, 2023), 86.; Brian S. Rosner and Roy E. Ciampa, *First Letter to the Corinthians* (Apollos, 2010), 424-425

The text at hand even seems to have a Hebraic parallel structure:[20]

A) I made myself a slave to all in order that I might gain more (19)

B) I became, to the Jews, as a Jew in order that I might gain Jews (20a)

B1) To those under the Torah, as under the Torah…To gain those under the Torah (20b)

C) To those outside of Torah, as outside of Torah…To gain those outside of Torah (21)

D) I became, to the weak, weak in order that I might gain the weak (22a)

A1) I have become all things to all, in order that I might in all circumstances save some of them (22b).

The next thing, besides the structure that presents itself, is that there only seems to be three groups of people that Paul is speaking about. This stands counter to the idea that there are four groups. The first group is Jews (B). This group of Jews is further designated as "under Torah" (B1). The group spoken of in line (C) are those "outside of Torah." The next group is further specified as "weak" (D).

Logically speaking how can Paul become a Jew? He was already a Jew. It is well-known that Paul never renounced his Jewishness (Acts 19:34; 21:39; 22:3; Phil 3:4-6).[21] Thus, Paul cannot truly "become" a Jew, as he already holds that status. So how should this statement be

---

20   Tim Hegg, "All things to all men: Paul and the Torah in 1 Cor. 9:19-23," https://torahresource.com/all-things-to-all-men/ (Accessed April 13, 2023). My analysis differs slightly from Hegg's here. He identifies 2 groups, whereas I find three. Hegg's chiastic structure is A, B, B1, C, C1, A1.

21   Hegg, "All Things to All Men," Torah Resource, 6. https://tr-pdf.s3-us-west-2.amazonaws.com/articles/all-things-to-all-men.pdf (Accessed January 5, 2023).

understood by interpreters? The answer is found in (B1), where Paul clarifies by adding the phrase "those under the Law/Torah" to specify the group he is referring to. It is this phrase, "under Torah," that really needs to be understood in order to ascertain the meaning of the text. It is my contention that it should, primarily, be understood as being under the condemnation of the Torah (Rom. 7:13; 8:1). However, Paul is also particularly interested in contrasting the Law of Christ with the oral law and ancestral traditions.[22] Therefore, the phrase *hupo nomon* is indicative of those who are reliant on the Law, primarily the status of the flesh and adherence to the oral law, to bring about salvation. The Party of the Circumcision thought that Jewish identity, as described in the Law, is what allowed them participation in the kingdom of God. To Paul, these Jews are under the condemnation of the Torah, because they do not have the faith that is supposed to precede faithful obedience as the Jewish law was in violation of the written Law of Moses. This fact is precisely why Paul then adds that he himself is not under Torah. It seems that Paul wants to make it abundantly clear that neither Jewish status nor works of the Law (primarily circumcision) were the basis for justification. In this case we see that Paul is neither under the condemnation of the written Torah, having been set free from the Law of Sin, but also that he is not under the oral torah as well as a result. Furthermore, from the analysis earlier, we know that Paul and James clearly understand that forsaking Moses is considered apostasy. So, it would be quite disingenuous for Paul to say that he is forsaking Moses to the ekklesia at Corinth, but then tell James that he did not commit apostasy from the Mosaic Law in Acts 21. The point is, in Paul's view, oral Law and Jewish status cannot bring about righteous standing before God. Justification before God

---

22   Cha, *Misunderstanding Galatians*, 17.

is through faith. Without actual faith and belief in the Messiah, those that continue to believe this are under the Torah because the Torah is condemning them in their sin. So then, what can it mean that Paul became "under Torah?" Paul himself says that he became under law, but he was not himself under law, so that he could win some under law. Assuming that when he says, "under law," Paul is referring to the condemnation of the Mosaic Law, the verse would read as follows when broken down into its primary components:

1. To those under the condemnation of the Torah I became under the condemnation of the Torah,
2. though not myself under the condemnation of the torah,
3. so I might win some under the condemnation of the Torah.

Admittedly, the writing is "difficult to understand" (cf. 2 Pet. 3:16). Once a person is freed from the condemnation of the Torah, they cannot become under its condemnation again, unless of course they apostatize (but we know that Paul is not an apostate, for this violates Acts 21). So, it seems at first glance that propositions 1 and 2 are contradictory. One cannot be "under" and "not under" simultaneously. Additionally, in terms of soteriology, if being under the Torah is the same as not being saved, how could a person who is not saved then save someone? It would be like a lifeguard trying to rescue a drowning person in extremely hazardous water by throwing himself into the water instead of throwing a life-preserver. A drowning person cannot rescue another drowning person. Therein lies the rub. Paul's relinquishing of personal freedom and his sacrificial attitude is what is on display. Taking Paul's earlier words in Rom. 9:3 at face value, he would consider himself accursed, separated from Christ (i.e., under the condemnation of the Torah) in order to save his brethren. Paul demonstrates this sacrificial heart by even submitting himself to the halachic rulings in order to maintain fellowship with the Jews. In fact, Paul's continued submission to the synagogue authorities *up to the point of lashings* (2 Cor. 11:24) makes his stance abundantly clear.[23] By forfeiting his freedom, he submitted himself to be under the law of their *dogma* so that he could win some of them to faith because they were, in fact, the ones still under the condemnation of the written Law.[24] Submitting to the synagogue authorities was Paul's way of showing that he would actually die and be damned for his brothers. He did this so that he could reach the unbelieving Jews, who were without Christ. Perhaps this is the true biblical version of the Conciliatory Theory, as Paul did everything in his power to maintain association and unity with his Jewish brethren, being beaten five times to remain in fellowship, in the hopes that they would find the Messiah.

What about the other groups mentioned in 1 Corinthians 9? Remember the idea that was prevalent in the first-century Judaisms, that Gentiles must become Jewish to partake in the Kingdom of

---

23   Nanos makes a relevant argument from 2 Cor. 11:24, which connects, according to him, directly to Rom. 13 and the synagogue authorities being the ones actually bearing the sword, as opposed to the anachronistic interpretation of secular government. Although commentary on Rom. 13 is outside the scope of this book, Nanos, quoting E.P. Sanders, underscores how integrally connected the Jesus movement and the synagogue must have been for Paul to have received these lashings. Given that Paul submitted to lashings and that he and Messiah were encouraging believers to submit to those in the seat of Moses, though not to certain halakhic rulings (coerced circumcision or other traditions that violate Moses), it would have put many believers afoul of the ruling elite. Nonetheless, with the emerging separation of dogma, it seems, as Sanders points out, that "punishment implies inclusion." See Mark Nanos, *The Mystery of Romans*, 311. Nanos quotes E.P. Sanders, *Paul, the Law, and the Jewish people* (Fortress Press, 1985), 192.

24   Cha, *Misunderstanding Galatians*, 17; Yosef Koelner and Jeffrey Seif underscore that Paul "operated within clear halachic boundaries in his efforts to win both Jew and Gentile in Messiah." Koelner and Seif, *Corinthians*, 83.

Heaven? This becomes very important in understanding verse 21 and the reason behind Paul's use of *anomos* and *ennomos*. 1 Corinthians 9:21 says, "To those who are without law (*anomos*), as without law (*anomos*), though not being without the law of God (*anomos Theos*) but under the law of Christ (*ennomos Christos*), so that I might win those who are without law (*anomos*)."

Firstly, and most importantly, here is the explicit instruction that Paul is not without the Law of God (*anomos Theos*) and that the law of God is synonymous with the necessary, direct, and proper execution of that law, which is the Law of Christ (*ennomos Christos*).[25] Since Paul is not without the Law of God, any notion that Paul set aside the Torah should be put to rest. Secondly, the very phrase "without Torah" has substantial usage within the traditional synagogue, in the LXX, and was later codified in Talmudic writings, which describe the Gentiles and apostate Jews as transgressors of the Law of God and who are thus described as "anomos" or outside of the covenant promises of God.[26] In Ephesians 2:11-12 and 4:17-32, Paul even partially confirms this prevailing view of First-century Judaism, that unbelieving Gentiles are outside the covenants of God, as they are cut off, without hope, and walk in a manner that is *anomos* (especially Eph. 4:18-32). So, it seems here that Paul is showing himself to be fully lawful while reach-

---

25 *Ennomos* was used during the first century to define the proper law and practice of those who conformed their lives to it. See Liddell & Scott, *Lexicon*, "ennomos." This understanding is confirmed and found in the LXX in Sirach (Ecclesiasticus) prologue v. 10.

26 1 Macc. 7:5; 9:23, 58, 69; 11:25; 14:14.; t. Demai 2:5 says, "A proselyte who took upon himself all the obligations of the Torah except for one item, they do not receive him." In this case, the primary contention being circumcision. This would render the gentile convert in the eyes of the Party of the Circumcision as anomos and still outside the Covenants of the Promise.

ing out to those who are fully without Torah and are outside of the covenant promises. The addition of *ennomos Christos* is to show that Paul is walking in a manner like Christ, which is the proper and pure manifestation of the Law of God. This stands in contrast to other laws or rulings, particularly those of the rabbinic authorities, which might have forbade association with those Gentiles who were *anomos* and even considered "enemies of God."[27] So, for instance, Paul might have to enter the house of a pagan to share the Good News. Paul could go and associate, while remaining fully Lawful and true to the Torah. In other words, although the unbelieving Gentiles are without the Torah, Paul would stay within the confines of the Torah, so that he could win some who were without Christ and his Law. Given the specificity, it almost seems that Paul is trying to show that he is not an apostate from Moses in his teaching of both Jew and Greek in Corinth. In short, Paul would not sin for evangelistic success and, considering the text in Acts 21, he is avoiding the charge of apostasy altogether, not to mention seemingly beginning the fulfillment Isaiah's prophesy to bring the *neichor* to faith and obedience (Is. 56:3, 6; 60:10; 61:5).[28]

Having identified the two groups he is trying to win (unbelieving Jews and unbelieving Gentiles), how can one understand what being "weak" entails? From the book of 1 Corinthians, weakness seems to be a relevant theme, especially in the preceding chapter and proceeding chapter about relinquishing freedom in regard to foods found in

---

27   C.G. Montegiore and H.M.J Loewe, eds., *A Rabbinic Anthology*), 570. Interestingly, should we view the enemies of God in the Tanakh, neichor/nochri (see Josh. 24:20; Jer. 5:19; 8:19; Mal. 2:11; 2 Sam 22:45-46; Neh 9:2; 13:30; 1Kings 11:1; Ezra 10:2; Prov. 2:16; 5:20; 7:5; 23:27), it is only in Isaiah's prophecy where the neichor (primarily Gentile enemies) are brought into Israel's covenant and participating in the Sabbath as a mark of the covenant. See Is. 56:3, 6; 60:10; 61:5.

28   Note especially Is. 56:6, which has the foreigners participating in the Sabbath.

the pagan temple district. Paul is identifying with the group that are labeled "weak" because if the context is about relinquishing freedom, Paul would gladly relinquish his liberty to eat clean meats, for those who considered any meats purchased near the pagan temples to be unclean. In fact, Paul says that if one knows that they are sacrificed to idols, "Do not eat" (1 Cor. 10:28). Eating meat sacrificed to idols is a violation of the First Jerusalem Council's rulings. The broader context in Corinth suggests that some within the congregation were concerned about the marketplace meats being considered unclean due to their proximity to pagan practices and the potential that they originated from pagan sacrifices. Paul also gives the injunction about marketplace meats, that if one is ignorant of its status, do not ask (1 Cor. 10:25). The point is, in keeping with the theme, if someone is weak in conscience, Paul, though not actually weak in faith or conscience, would willingly relinquish his freedom to support those who are weaker. In other words, just because it is lawful to eat clean marketplace meat does not mean it is profitable for the whole community (1 Cor. 10:23). In this way, Paul can truly say that he became as weak, fully identifying with that group, although the text shows that Paul is definitely not weak in conscience. To the contrary, the relinquishing of freedom shows monumental strength of character.

To conclude this series of verses, Paul says, "I have become all things to all men, so that I may by all means save some. I do all things for the sake of the gospel, so that I may become a fellow partaker of it." Using his own life as the example (imitate him as he imitates Christ), Paul underscores the very sacrificial love of Messiah. He not only submits himself to the authorities of the synagogue, but would also go amongst the nations to win some. In short, he sacrificed his very freedom for the sake of the gospel. This is what the Conciliatory Theory should be. The passage was never about the continuity of the

Mosaic Law at all, but rather Paul's radical obedience to the Law and the Great Commission as taught by Messiah (*ennomos Christos*). The Jews who rejected the Messiah are still under the condemnation of the Torah. Their reliance on the status of the flesh and oral law rendered them lost, just like the unbelieving Gentile. To that end, it seems that if the Law is the standard of righteousness and the defining standard of sin, and that Paul walks orderly keeping the Torah (Acts 21), there is no way that Paul would commit a sin (violating the Torah) so that "grace can abound" to the Gentiles (cf. Rom. 6:1-2). In other words, Paul is not free to eat swine in the presence of a Gentile for evangelistic success. The bottom line is that if Paul is violating the Torah to win Gentiles, he would be sinning so that grace would abound to the Gentiles. This is nothing short of apostasy, and would necessitate a third Jerusalem Council to finally convict Paul of apostasy. Is not the goal of the nation of Israel as a whole, and Paul in particular, to bring the nations into alignment with the established Word of God, not bring the Word of God into alignment with the lawless Gentiles (cf. Rom. 15:18)? Here at Corinth, Paul was willing to sacrifice his freedom so that he could win unbelieving Jews and unbelieving Gentiles. Furthermore, Paul is also willing to sacrifice even his freedom within the Law so that those of weaker consciences would not stumble. Paul is ready and willing to sacrifice any perceived freedom he has to win either Jew or Greek and promote unity within the community. He is willing to do all lawful things for the sake of the gospel, even sacrificing his body to lashings or forfeiting his own salvation (2 Cor. 11:24; Rom. 8:18; 9:3)! Never, at any time, does Paul agree to violate the Law of Moses to have evangelistic success for those who have not been exposed to the Law of Moses. As Paul says elsewhere, "Are we to continue in sin so that grace my increase? Far from it! How shall we who died to sin still live in it?" (Rom. 6:1-2) Therefore, it is quite unlikely that this text is speaking to bilateral orthopraxy, violating the Torah for evangelism, or the notion that Paul is merely performing his Nazirite Vow in Acts 21 as a conciliatory act. In fact, Paul's actions at Corinth are more indicative of reconciliation and genuine unity as opposed to conciliatory. Paul is desperately, up to the point of death, trying to bring Jew and Gentile together and to build up the body in Messiah. Conciliation means *changing* doctrine to accommodate or compromise, whereas reconciliation is joining together under a single banner, that is Christ and his Law.

What Does This Do to the Conciliatory Theory as Commonly Understood?

Based on the analysis above, Paul never, at any time, taught the Jews or the Gentiles to apostatize from Moses. The Nazirite Vow of Acts 21 was not a conciliatory gesture toward the Jews; ; it was to show Paul's radical adherence to the Law (cf. Rom. 3:31). Paul told James the truth. Being "all things to all men" is simply a rabbinic rhetorical device that Paul used to show his willingness to sacrifice himself for the sake of Christ and to fulfill the Abrahamic covenant to bless all the nations. This sacrificial love is, of course, the true definition of conciliatory, but in reality it is more in line with reconciliation of people toward God and into the covenants. Paul is willing, by all lawful means available to him, to unite two distinct groups as one in Messiah, fulfilling the promise to Abraham to bless all the nations of the earth. For God is not faithful unless all the nations of the earth are blessed, according to the Abrahamic covenant. Paul believes that the Tree of Life (the Torah and the Messiah) are healing for the nations (cf. Rev. 22:2). Therefore, one can conclude that in no way does Paul preach apostasy from Moses, but rather he underscores his desire (Christ's desire) to see both Jew and Greek become partakers in the

Covenants of the Promise. The Torah serves as the rules for the marriage covenant and the fundamental promise of the New Covenant (Jer. 31:31-34). There is no distinction between Jew and Greek, and there is but one God, one Lord, one Law, one faith, and one baptism for the Jew and the Sojourner among them (Num. 15:16; Is. 56:6-7; Acts 15:9; Rom. 3:22; 10:12; Col. 3:11). A compromise or appeasement theory, motivated by prudential self-interest in response to either Jewish Christians, unbelieving Jews, or Jewish nationalists, as Polhill argues, would portray Paul and James as doctrinal chameleons at best. This perspective also contradicts other scriptures that emphasize the unity of one people (Rom. 11).[29] In this vein, Acts 21 would be the only instance in the Bible where men verbally ordained by God—apostles who witnessed the risen Lord—conceded doctrinal ground to appease those who were in error, without it being corrected.[30] It is my contention, that this is not the case. Rather, considering the fact that the Tanakh explicitly says there is One Law and One God, and that the Apostles declare there is only one faith and one baptism, and that Adonai is the God to both the Greek and the Jew, the Scriptures seem to preclude any notion of appeasement or compromise.

It seems more likely that as the Gospel spread and all nations of the earth were blessed (Gal. 3:8; Gen. 12:3), the Law would also extend to the nations, thereby fulfilling Deuteronomy 4:6-8 and the promise of the New Covenant. The prophets also were inspired to write that *through* the work of Israel and her Messiah, the Gentiles would come to know and obey the Torah (Is. 2:1-4; Mic 4:1-5). Is not

---

29   John B. Polhill, *Acts*, 449–450.

30   Peter's hypocrisy is the only instance we have of an apostle doing wrong, and he is corrected by God himself (Acts 10-11) and Paul (Gal. 2). Nowhere are James and Paul corrected by insisting Gentiles hear Moses Preached (Acts 15:21) nor by continuing in Temple sacrifices (Acts 21).

the New Covenant prophesied to write the Torah on the heart which results in faithful obedience from heart of love toward God?[31] It is my contention that when Gentiles believe in the Messiah they become full covenant members into all the covenants of God, which cannot be annulled or abrogated once initiated.[32] As Paul says elsewhere, the Gentiles were excluded from the Politeia of Israel and strangers to the covenants of the promise (Eph. 2:13). So instead of seeing compromise, conciliatory attempts, or appeasement, I propose that Acts 21 is

---

31 Jer. 31:31-33; Hos. 1:10; Rom. 9:25. As it is written in several forms, "If you love me, keep my commandments." Ex. 20:3-6; Deut. 5:8-10; 7:9-11; 10:12-13; 11:1, 13-14, 22-23; 19:8-9; 30:16; Josh. 22:5; Dan. 9:4; Neh. 1:5-6; Jn. 14:15, 21; 1 Jn. 5:2-3; 2 Jn. 1:6.

32 Paul says in Gal. 3:15-17 that covenants cannot be set aside once they are ratified. A potential defeater for the position however is found directly after in Gal. 3:19. To begin, there are significant textual disagreements surrounding this verse and the syntax can be read in different ways. As Staples points out, a reading of τῶν πράξεων instead of τῶν παραβόσεων has earlier historical attestation. Thus, the translation is more akin to "Law of Deeds." These additional halakhic laws to the Torah were "added," which brings close similarity to Gal. 3:10 and the idiom of "Works of the Law," which has already been shown to be the denominational markers between sects of Judaism as typified by its use at Qumran (1QS v. 21, 23 and 4QFlor. i.7, 4QMMT). See Staples, "Law of Deeds," in Gal 3:19a, 126-127. So, Paul may not actually be addressing the Biblical Law of God, but rather Pharisaical Law. See Wallace, *Exegetical Syntax*, 306, 308; Dunn, *Galatians*, 189.; Cha, *Misunderstanding Galatians*, 169.; Keener, *Galatians*, 281. Most importantly, should the text be read as Mosaic abolition, it is my contention that this directly contradicts the Messiahs own words in Mt. 5:17-19. In this regard, Longenecker concludes that the traditional view of Galatians 3:19 would be a wild departure from any form of Judaism and the teaching of Messiah as there are no other sources within Judaism that speak of the Law this way, nor are there any other Biblical sources that speak of the Law as a temporary structure. See Longenecker, *Galatians*, 139. In other words, Gal. 3:19 is better interpreted as saying that the purpose of the Jewish law (law of Deeds), was to function temporarily, until the Messiah would come. These human messengers were the intermediaries who established what Judaism became. When the Messiah came, he brought the Law of Christ, which is the proper interpretation of the Mosaic Law/Law of God. Eph. 2:13. (Plural covenants, a singular promise)

demonstrating radical reconciliation, bringing all the nations and the Jews into alignment with the Word of God as taught by Messiah. Paul's mission is to bring radical obedience to the Gentiles, while James and Peter were attempting the same with the unbelieving Jews.[33] This obedience of faith is not following the unlawful traditions of first-century Judaism, but following the Law of Christ.[34] This nuanced message was misunderstood by many in the diaspora. To their credit, if Paul had been teaching apostasy, he would have been guilty of violating Deuteronomy 13:1-4. However, to demonstrate that Paul did not break this commandment, he participates in Temple service, at the very least paying for the Nazirite vow, if not also partaking in it himself. To interpret Acts 21 as involving compromise or appeasement is to project assumptions onto the text, particularly drawing from 1 Corinthians 9 and Galatians, which may not be justified. This approach overlooks Paul's nuanced use of *nomos* and his idiomatic phrases like "works of the law" and "under law," as well as the textual distinctions emphasizing oral law over Biblical Law. These issues, along with the misinterpretation of Peter's vision in Acts 10-11, reveal significant historical and hermeneutical weaknesses in the Conciliatory Theory. It struggles to maintain consistency when compared to the words of Christ, the prophets, and the apostles' writings within their historical context.

---

33   Their actions seem to be the inauguration and beginning fulfillment of the New Covenant promises, ultimately to culminate and come to full fruition upon the return of the Messiah and Millennial reign.

34   The promise is granted by faith. The Law is how people of faith act and abide in grace.

CHAPTER 4
OTHER OBJECTIONS

Having highlighted the deficiencies and misinterpretations within both the Transitory and Conciliatory theories, there are still a few remaining objections that need to be addressed.

The Moral, Civil, Ceremonial Distinction: Paul's Emphasis on Moral Commandments

A potential reply to the theology presented in this book is that there is a distinction between the moral, civil, and ceremonial law.[1] I have already addressed many of the assumptions that ground the supposed moral, civil, and ceremonial distinction in the previous chapters.[2] However, even if one accepts the assumption that the Law of God can be divided into these distinct parts, the tight interweaving of these components in the Tanakh makes such theological tweezing highly difficult at best and would be wrought with disagreements among various sects and traditions. For example, Exodus 22:19-29 contains regulations that span moral, civil, and ceremonial aspects of the Law, often overlapping between these categories:

> Whoever lies with an animal shall surely be put to death
> [*moral*]. He who sacrifices to any god, other than to the
> LORD alone shall be utterly destroyed [*Moral, Ceremonial*].

---

1   *Westminster Confession of Faith* (1646); *London Baptist Confession* XIX (1677).

2   Primarily the misreading of Acts 10-11, Mk. 7:19, Paul's nuanced use of *nomos* (as well as "under law"), the idiomatic identification of "Works of the Law," the historical and social reasons for a shift from Sabbath to Sunday, the eschatological reapplication of the Mosaic Law, etc.

You shall not wrong a stranger or oppress him, for you were strangers in the land of Egypt [*Moral, Civil*]. You shall not afflict any widow or orphan [*Moral, Civil*]. If you afflict him at all, and if he does cry out to Me, I will surely hear his cry; and my anger will be kindled, and I will kill you with the sword and your wives shall be come widow and your children fatherless [*Moral, Civil*]. If you lend money to My people, to the poor among you, you are not to act as a creditor to him; you shall not charge him interest. If you ever take your neighbor's cloak as a pledge, you are to return it to him before the sun sets, for that is his only covering; it is his cloak for his body. What else shall he sleep in? And it shall come about that when he cries out to Me, I will hear him, for I am gracious [*Civil, Moral*]. You shall not curse God, nor curse a ruler of your people [*Moral, Civil*]. You shall not delay the offering from your harvest and your vintage [*Moral, Ceremonial*]. The firstborn of your sons shall give to me [*Moral, Ceremonial*].
—Exodus 22:19-29

As we can see, the scriptures do not provide an ascertainable way to distinguish between the moral, civil, and ceremonial laws. Instead, these laws are interconnected, woven together through the narrative, and seem to intertwine individual obligations with both collective and religious contexts.

Another demonstration of this is found in Leviticus 19, which starts with the command to "be holy." The chapter then details what "holiness" means, covering a range of instructions such as loving one's neighbor (*Moral, Civil*), practicing impartiality in court (*Moral, Civil*), refraining from holding grudges (*Moral*), and keeping the Sabbath (Moral, Civil, Ceremonial). These instructions serve multiple roles within the community of God's people. While they are all moral in nature, they also bleed into other categories.

To that end the commands for Sabbath are particularly difficult to separate into moral, civil, and ceremonial constructs. Exodus 31:12 says, "this is a sign between Me and you throughout your generations that you may know that I am the LORD who sanctifies you." As in, any abolition, profaning, or disregarding the Sabbath would be to disregard one of the means by which God intends to make persons holy. Furthermore, disregarding the Sabbath and its instructions (not buying, selling, or working people or animals) incurs the death penalty in Exodus 31:14. Lastly, the Sabbath was instituted at the beginning of creation to mark the division of the week and, together with the moon, sun, and stars, to help determine the years and festivals. It also illustrates that even the agent of creation, Jesus Christ, rested from his work (cf. Heb. 1:2). Therefore, the Sabbath has moral (being made holy), civil (no buying or selling and punishable by death), and ceremonial (determining times, seasons, and holy days) components, which cannot be practically separated.[3]

Furthermore, when the biblical authors reference the Torah, they often use language that emphasizes its unity. For instance, in Romans 7:9-11, Paul uses the singular term "commandment" to show that the entire unity of the Torah reveals both sin and righteousness.[4] Here is seems that Paul is continuing the use of unitary language that was started by Moses and was later used by Joshua and David.[5] What is

---

3   Part of this ceremonial aspect likewise has a moral connection, as the people of God are morally obligated to "remember" why the ceremonies are actually done: (1) Creation, (2) Redemption, and (3) Sanctification.

4   This singular use is often used in conjunction with plural Torah synonyms such as "commandments," "statutes," and "precepts."

5   See Ex. 24:12; Deut. 6:1; Josh. 22:5; Ps. 19:8.

more, this approach of dividing the Law into moral, civil, and ceremonial categories is troubled when trying to synthesize this position with Jesus's words in Matthew 5:18. Christ does not make a distinction between any particular laws, but rather references the whole Law as a singular unit.

The Moral Emphasis in Paul and Torah Realism

There is no question that Paul often emphasizes the moral side of the commandments in unique ways. For instance, in 1 Corinthians 9:9 and 1 Timothy 5:18, Paul cites Deuteronomy 25:4, which states, "You shall not muzzle the ox while it is threshing." He applies this civil/moral commandment using a lesser-to-greater argument to prove that those who make their living by preaching the Gospel should be paid. In other words, even rules that could be considered civil or even ceremonial have moral components—that is, there are no rigid boundaries between the moral, civil, and ceremonial categories. The literal command applies as well as the moral command. Likewise, moral principles can and ought to take precedence over ceremonial and civil laws in some cases. In another case of a lesser-to-greater argument, Yeshua says, "How much more valuable then is a man than a sheep! So then, it is lawful to do good on the Sabbath" (Mt. 12:12; cf. Mk. 3:4, Lk. 6:9). So, in this regard, there is a normative moral, civil, and ceremonial command in the Sabbath, but also some cases could arise where other moral commands (such as preserving life—e.g., loving your neighbor) would take precedence over what would normally be a time of rest and sanctification. These are obvious legal exceptions, and the Torah itself indicates that there are times when certain laws do not apply, even in ceremonial situations where they typically would (see, e.g., Lev. 10:16-20). Likewise, Christ emphasizes that the Torah prioritizes matters of justice, mercy, faithfulness, and love of God, identifying these as the "weightier" matters of the Law (Mt. 23:23; Lk. 11:42). Therefore, one can say that any directly moral commandment, or a moral precedent derived from other potential forms of commandments, are the primary focus of the Law.

Given the emphasis on moral aspects of the Law by both Paul and Christ, combined with the assumptions and interpretive commitments of the Conciliatory or Transitory theories discussed earlier, it is understandable how Paul's writings could be seen as leaning toward an exclusive focus on moral law or expressing a degree of indifference (adiaphora) toward the ceremonial rites. For instance, Fruchtenbaum says, "Just as freedom from the law means freedom also to keep certain aspects of the law...such as the Jewish holy days."[6] He continues, "He is free in Christ from these things, but he is also free in Christ to observe such things that do not violate clear New Testament teaching."[7] What Fruchtenbaum is saying here is dependent upon his understanding of passages already covered,[8] so there is no need to rehash them here. But in essence, his theory suggests that Paul (and the other apostles) participated in the Temple service, even though they understood that it was ultimately not necessary. The implication is that these rituals could be performed if one wants to, but there was no obligation to do so if one chooses not to.

To address this position, it is helpful, ironically, to begin with Eschatology. Assuming premillennial eschatology, if Christ's death and resurrection were effectual for abolishing the ceremonial laws, thus explaining Paul's potential adiaphora, then this efficaciousness would continue into eternity, would it not? Is not Christ's effective-

---

6   Fruchtenbaum, *Israelology*, 724.

7   Ibid., 909.; See also Ryrie, *Basic Theology*, XII, Ch.75, 15.

8   Rom. 14, Acts 10-11, 20:7; Gal. 3:10, 17-19; 1 Cor. 9.

ness perpetually effective? Hence, the question is raised: why do the prophets continually proclaim not only the Law's continuance but also its observance by both ethnic Jews and those from among the nations? A main theme in the prophets is the proclamation, not only of a victorious Messiah, but also the continuity of both civil and ceremonial laws in the earthly reign of the Messiah.[9] It is further said that the nations will not receive rain should they fail to observe *ceremonial commands* for the Festival of Sukkot (Zech. 14:18).[10] The key point is that if Christ had truly abolished those ceremonial or civil laws through his death and resurrection, it would be impossible for them to be reinstated according to Scripture. What was accomplished at Golgotha was final, irrevocable, and cannot be overturned. One could also say that Christ precludes this before his death saying that he did not come to abolish the Law (Mt. 5:17-20). What seems to be one of the overarching themes of Jesus's salvific purpose was to actually secure his faithful bride's obedience to the Law (replacing the heart of stone with a heart of flesh).[11] The (super)natural outworking of this

---

9   Ez. 36:24-38. "I will cause them to walk in my statutes…" Ezekiel elsewhere describes the laws for charging interest (18:17) and keeping the Sabbath and the festivals (20:13, 16: 44:24). Other examples abound. See Is 56:6-7, which has Gentiles observing the Sabbath and holding fast to the Covenant in the Temple ("House of Prayer"), making burnt offerings and sacrifices. Zech. 14:16 has all the nations going up to observe the Feast of Sukkot.

10   This verse is particularly interesting as it has a collective civil judgement against a nation resulting in no rain, thus showing how not obeying a ceremonial command is a *moral* failure.

11   Jer. 31:31-33; Ez. 11:19, 36:26-27. "I will put my Spirit within you and cause you to walk in My statutes, and you will be careful to observe My ordinances." In other words, Paul's (and Moses's) emphasis on circumcision of the heart is synonymous with the faithful obedience to God's word, which is the result of faith. Hab. 2:4; Heb. 11:28 says, "By faith he kept the Passover…" Heb. 11:32-33 says, "And what more shall I say? For time will fail me if I tell of Gideon, Barak, Samson, Jephthah, of David and Samuel and the

salvation is *living* by faith and doing the works of that faith.[12] As such,

prophets, who by faith conquered kingdoms, performed acts of righteousness, obtained promises..." (Italics for emphasis – "acts" in 11:33 is italicized in NASB95).

12   The righteous shall live by faith (Hab. 2:4; Rom. 1:17). James 2:17 says, "Even so faith, if it has no works, is dead, being by itself." To that end, the ontology of faith consists of an intellectual/emotive component, but is also combined with works for it to actually be alive. This does not mean however that one can be justified by the Law (Rom. 3:28), for all have fallen short of that. However, the fact one cannot be declared righteous by the law does not mean that the standard and covenants by which we fell short no longer apply through Christ. Rather, the salvific act of faith should be transformative as to bring full alignment to those covenants (Eph. 2:11-15). For even Abraham, by faith, obeyed the Lord as demonstrated by keeping, "My charge (*mismeret*), My commandments (*mitzvah*), My statutes (*huqqa*), and My Laws (*Torah*)" (Gen. 26:5). As such, Michael Bird demonstrates that justification and sanctification are linked logically rather than conceptually. With that integral link, "obedience, faithfulness, righteousness, and love are imperatives that grow out of saving faith." Bird, *The Saving Righteousness of God: Studies on Paul, Justification and the New Perspective* (Wipf and Stock, 2007), 111. However, Bird's analysis and use of the word "imperative" marks a necessary tension of works/faith synergy. For "imperative" brings an essential and obligatory requirement of works. That is, faith's necessary response to grace is submission to God's righteous requirements for living (Rom. 8:7; Lk. 14:27-33). It does not matter if this submission is for a few hours (e.g., the rebel crucified with Christ) or over the course of a longer life. Furthermore, Mt. 7:23 and Heb. 6:4-6; 10:26-27 (See also Rev. 2-3) are of particular importance as they demonstrate that deeds, as defined by the Word of God, are how people are judged by God. So how is this tension released? It seems that much of the tension can be resolved if one views grace (*charis*) more like patronage. That is, redemption is granted by grace alone, but in the patronage model, the one receiving the benefit returns the favor in a system of reciprocal and faithful service, as the gift received was given solely because of the undeserved good will of the patron. In return, the receiver of said grace must perform any and all service demanded of them because those receiving the grace could in no way obtain it or attain it on their own (e.g., the way a patron might provide capital, like providing a ship for an explorer or trader). The beneficiary of that grace is now obligated to the patron in all things, giving them preference. With the case at hand, "free" voyages or transit, and priority when using said ship and perhaps 10% of all profits and increase. In much the same way, since all believers in all times are granted grace, the demands of that grace, accordingly, are repentance and faithful obedience to the

it is quite a mistake to view grace through the lens of late medieval piety via the Protestant polemics of trying to earn salvation through pious works. Rather, there is a significant thrust in the ancient world that grace has a direct and necessary response from the receiver of grace.[13] As DeSilva notes:

> As in asymmetrical relationship between human patrons and clients, those of lower station do not presume that they can match the favors they have received from a much greater and better-resourced patron, but rather devote themselves to making the fullest return that lies within *their power* (and that, too, supported here by God's sustaining help).[14]

This becomes evident in Pauline ecclesiology and eschatological judgment as he develops a case for removing either Jew or Gentile from the community. In 1 Corinthians 5:13, Paul exhorts the community to purge the wicked from among yourselves.[15] The language Paul employs here comes mostly from Deuteronomy.[16] The contexts in these texts from Deuteronomy seem to be indicating numerous issues, such as idolatry (Deut. 13:5, 17:7), *any iniquity or any sin* and malicious witnesses (Deut. 19:15-17), the drunkard and rebellious son (Deut. 21:21), sexual immorality (Deut. 22:21, 22, 24), as well

---

terms of the covenant of that grace in all facets of life since this grace has gifted life itself. See David A. DeSilva, *Honor, Patronage, Kinship, and Purity: Unlocking New Testament Culture* (Grand Rapids, MI: IVP, 2022), 137-184.

13   Aristotle, *Nicomachean Ethics* 8.14.4; Seneca, *de Beneficiis* 2.24.4.

14   DeSilva, *Honor, Patronage, Kinship, and Purity*, 161. Emphas added.

15   Christ's method for this is laid out in Mt. 18:15-17.

16   Deut. 13:5; 17:7; 19:19; 21:21; 22:21, 22, 24; 24:7; Judg. 20:13.

as kidnapping and human trafficking (Deut. 24:7).[17] With that, the surrounding context in Corinth seems to show the only thing lacking in their sin is the kidnapping (1 Cor. 5:1, 11). In Corinth, the way Paul executes the purging of the wicked is to hand these people over to Satan for the destruction of their flesh so that their spirit may be saved in in the day of the Lord Jesus (1 Cor. 5:5; cf. 1 Tim. 1:20).[18] In addition to this, the author of Hebrews as well as Christ's words, seem to temper the potential conclusion that being delivered to Satan for the destruction of the flesh will automatically guarantee an eschatological salvation (Heb. 6:6; Heb. 10:26-31; Mt. 7:23). In other words, each man must be careful how he builds on Christ's foundation (1 Cor. 3:10-11). There are three possible outcomes of the fire in which one's works are judged. Gold, silver, or precious stones are refined and remain. Wood, hay, and stubble are burned up, yet that person is saved as through fire. However, Paul also says that destruction can also ensue, in 1 Cor. 3:17, that "If any man destroys/corrupts the temple of God, God will destroy him, for the Temple of God is holy, and that is what you are." In other words, abiding in holiness is a moral obligation with both ecclesiastical pragmatism and potential apostasy resulting in eschatological judgment, should one continue to practice willful sin thus causing a "shipwreck to their faith."[19]

This brings the argument back to the four essentials of Acts 15. The sins that require immediate purging are idolatry and sexual immorality, but these commands in no way negate the standing commandments surrounding ceremonial laws. For instance, foreigners wanting

---

17 See also Heb. 10:28. Interestingly, the author of Hebrews casts this verse in present tense.

18 I would place Judas Iscariot in this category as well (Jn. 13:27). This seems to show that temporal destruction and judgement need not necessarily lead to eschatological damnation.

19 As in continually and unrepentantly. See 1 Tim. 1:19.

to partake in the sacrificial components of the Passover must be circumcised.[20] It is here at the Temple service where I believe that Paul's moral emphasis to Gentile communities is confused with sacrificial adiaphora as opposed to a legal understanding of potential mootness in both civil and ceremonial cases.

Accordingly, first-century Judaism, in accordance with the provisions laid out in the Torah, had already developed ways to obey the commandments of God while in locations that were considerable distances from the Temple.[21] Other Rabbinic sources underscore the importance of being in the land and how it is tied to an ability to fulfill the commandments.[22] Deuteronomy 12:5 and 11 further clarifies this:

> But you shall seek the LORD at the place which the LORD
> your God will choose from all your tribes, to establish His
> name there for His dwelling, and there you shall come...
> then it shall come about that the place in which the LORD
> your God will choose for His name to dwell, there you shall

---

20 Ex. 12. These are the rules the Patron has made for worship in this way.

21 Keener, *Acts*, vol. 3, 635.; Deut. 12:21; 14:24; See b. Hullin 89b; 100b; Numbers Rabbah 10:13.

22 m. *Kellim* 1:6.; *Midrash Siferi, Re'eh* 80 says, "When they arrived in Tzidon, and remembered the Land of Israel, they lifted up their eyes and tears dripped from them, and they ripped their clothes and recited the verse, 'You shall inherit it, and settle in it, for in it you can observe all the laws." (Italics for emphasis – the verse is from Deut. 11:31) "They said: Settling in the land of Israel is equal in worth to all the commandments in the Torah combined. And they turned around and went back to the Land of Israel." *Deut. 11:31-32 actually says, "For you are about to cross the Jordan to go in to possess the land which the LORD your God is giving you and you shall possess it and live in it, and you shall be careful to do all the statutes and the judgments which I am setting before you today."

> bring all that I command you: your burnt offerings and your
> sacrifices, your tithes and the contribution of your hand, and
> all your choice votive offerings which you will vow to the
> LORD.
> —Deuteronomy 12:5, 11

In short, *full* observance of the ceremonial commandments is geographically dependent and requires a functioning Temple/Mishkan and Levitical priesthood. In other words, obligation is *geographically contextual* and based on *capacity for observance.*[23] If these conditions are not met for the portions of the Torah that outline ceremonial or civil structures then there is no concrete obligation, based on the word of God, to do them. What is more, it might be sin should one attempt to perform them without the appropriate structures in place. In other words, *ought implies can.* An excellent example of this is Daniel, who despite being in exile, continued to pray toward Jerusalem three times daily, indicative of the sacrificial times (evening, morning, and noon), but did not perform the actual sacrificial service (Dan. 6:10). Daniel likewise could observe the Kashrut laws, and Hananiah, Mishael, and Azariah did not commit idolatry (Dan. 1:8; 3:12). Another example is the apostles and Jesus's continued support and use of the Temple system despite the fact that the Ark of the Covenant was not present in Herod's Temple. Furthermore, civil structures are likewise upended or made moot by invading conquerors and the empires of Babylon, Persia, Assyria, Greece, and Rome. To that end, Paul's potential ceremonial adiaphora is not indicative of those portions of the Law as being unimportant for Gentiles. Quite the contrary, Paul's moral emphasis is indicative of a legal interpretation already common within

---

23   DeSilva, *Honor, Patronage, Kinship, and Purity*, 161.

Judaism. For if Paul's participation in the Nazirite vow means any-thing, as Keener demonstrates, it is "not simply a ruse to pretend that he allows Jews to keep the law but a fair portrayal of his own Jewish convictions."[24] However, contra Keener, it is not simply "Jewish convictions" about which Paul is concerned; rather, he is concerned with what the Word of God prescribes. As Jesus says, "Woe to you, scribes and Pharisees, hypocrites! For you tithe mint and dill and cummin, and have neglected the weightier provisions of the law: justice and mercy and faithfulness; but these are the things you should have done *without neglecting the others* (Mt. 23:23, emphasis added).

Therefore, understanding the fact that Torah observance of sacrificial and civil laws have necessary geographical and contextual limitations, and that the Law in and of itself does not serve in a forensic capacity for justification via grace (primarily that of circumcision), this motivates Paul to underscore the weightier provisions outlined in the Torah.[25] This emphasis of Paul, however, does not negate the ceremonial components, nor does it negate partial observance of the commands (as reflected in the intent of Deuteronomy 12:21 and 14:24). For Paul even says in 1 Corinthians 7:19, "Circumcision is nothing, and uncircumcision is nothing, but *what matters* is keeping the commandments of God."[26] If what matters is keeping the commandments of God, then Paul is underscoring that the Law of God has to be followed properly.[27] Accordingly, it seems that Paul outlines

---

24 Keener, *Acts*, vol. 3, 635-6.

25 Much like the prophets, whose contexts have fully functioning temple systems, also emphasized moral components.

26 Italics original in NASB 95.

27 Eph. 4:1; Phil. 1:27; Col. 1:10. Cicero famously wrote, "Law is the highest reason, rooted in nature, which commands things that must be done and prohibits the opposite." See *On the Commonwealth of and on the Laws*, 1.18. Applying this logic here, the Torah

what a proper response to grace entails. As such, he guides the early believers in Christ to act in a way that is befitting, otherwise they (and we) could be making an ungrateful response to the lovingkindness of the patron, thus potentially excluding us from future favors that have yet occurred.[28]

So then, contrary to the argument put forth by Fruchtenbaum and others, which asserts that observing the ceremonial aspects of the Law is a matter of adiaphora for Paul and merely optional for Gentiles, this view seems to be mistaken. The prophets suggest significant Gentile involvement in following the Law, and ecclesiastical discipline and potential judgment are tied to one's willing and continual violation of the Law (sin) after coming to the knowledge of the Messiah.[29] Furthermore, Paul's recognition of the geographical and historical limitations that prevent all the nations from physically being in Jerusalem to perform the ceremonial rites highlights his focus on the moral aspects of the Law. However, this in no way suggests that he viewed the ceremonial rites as optional for either Jews or Gentiles. Since the receivers of God's grace are in a place where they are physically, financially, politically, and geographically unable to give Adonai worship at the physical Temple, they are instructed to give the eternally beneficent patron due honor in all things that they are able to do. The human, as a mobile temple of God, is not to be defiled. As Paul writes elsewhere, "'Therefore, come out from their midst and be separate,' says the Lord. 'And do not touch what is unclean; and I will welcome you'" (2 Cor. 6:17; cf. Is. 52:11).

---

prescribes specific ways to observe its ceremonial ordinances—to do them outside of those contexts is prohibited. As it is written, "Scripture cannot be broken." Jn. 10:35.

28   DeSilva, *Honor, Patronage, Kinship, and Purity*, 184.

29   See Mark Kinzer, *Post-Missionary Messianic Judaism*, 152, 160.

CHAPTER 5

CONCLUSION: THE HERMENEUTICAL KEY

Acts 21 might be one of the most important historical narratives in the entire canon. The actions of the apostles, over thirty years after the resurrection of the Messiah, are a key hermeneutical foundation that not only confirms what the apostles believed, but also how they lived out their faith. Their actions reflect a robust commitment to the Messiah, expressed through adherence to the Mosaic Law—*Ennomos Christos* (the Law of Christ). This book has shown that, when examined closely, both the Transitory and Conciliatory approaches to Acts 21 do not hold up. In fact, these theories run counter to the entire biblical narrative. It is my contention that the entire New Testament is pointed toward the fact that Jesus's (Yeshua's) spirit produces the help required to do the deeds that he has commissioned us to do. It is by these works that we are judged. In short, we can dedicate our lives to study the requirements our loving Father has placed upon us and walk accordingly, or we can walk in apostasy and disobedience. This is what it means to be in a covenant relationship. With that, Messiah's primary mission was to cancel the curse of our *prior disobedience* and empower believers to obey fully. The goal of the Torah is the thorough and progressive transformation of the person via the power and gifts of God, ultimately leading them to become like Christ. Ironically, antinomian theologies that lean on the Conciliatory, Transitory, or, even worse, Contradictory theories, seek to support the notion that Christians are permitted to continually disregard several fundamental aspects of the Torah. They believe that Christ's spirit is empowering them to ignore, and in some cases, vehemently rebel against some, if not all, of the divinely given instructions. This is not only wrong but also inherently dangerous theology, as it stands against the very teachings of the apostles and the prophets before them, which consistently and continually call people back to the basic principles of the covenants.

This leads to the logical and hermeneutically consistent conclusion that the Continuous Theory has the most explanatory power, is less ad hoc, and makes the most sense of the biblical data. Based on the results above, the actions and statements of Paul and James in Acts 21, which occurred after the writing of Galatians, demonstrate that they view failure to follow Moses, as interpreted by the Messiah, as apostasy from the true faith. Faithful and proper obedience to the Torah, in their view, is the natural result of faithfulness to Christ. This fact alone is sufficient for the Pronomian Paradigm and serves as the hermeneutical key for unlocking other Pauline rhetoric. Although the established paradigm makes further explanation and exegesis of "difficult to understand" texts unnecessary, I maintain that, based on the admissions of Paul and James, any interpretation of an apostolic teaching that appears to speak against the continuity of the Torah is *automatically* mistaken. When one reads a text with Torah lenses in the Hebraic context, through Christ, all the texts that seem to speak against the Torah are actually speaking for the Torah.

POSTSCRIPT

While there are many more passages and ideas to discuss regarding the Apostles' and Yeshua's teachings on the continued validity of the Law of Moses, I hope that this excursion into Acts 21 and related texts has either strengthened your faith or perhaps challenged previously held assumptions and beliefs. It was an honor to contribute to this series of "Pocket Guide" books organized by David Wilber and Pronomian Publishing. This series is dedicated to addressing common objections to Torah observance today. I hope this series continues to provide a solid, accessible introduction to Pronomian Christianity and Messianic Judaism. Blessings and Shalom!

If you are interested in staying connected, please follow me on X (formerly Twitter): @thepronomian

BIBLIOGRAPHY

Arnold, Clinton E. *The Colossian Syncretism: The Interface Between Christianity and Folk Belief at Colossae.* Baker, 1996.

Bacchiocchi, Samuele. *From Sabbath to Sunday: A Historical Investigation of the Rise of Sunday Observation in Early Christianity.* Rome: The Pontifical Georgian University Press, 1977.

Bahnsen, Greg L. *Theonomy in Christian Ethics.* Phillipsburg, NJ: Presbyterian and Reformed Publishing Company, 1984.

Barnett, Paul W. *Jesus and the Logic of History.* Edited by DA Carson. Vol. 3. New Studies in Biblical Theology. IVP, 1997.

Barrett, C.K.A. *Acts: A Critical and Exegetical Commentary on the Acts of the Apostles.* T&T Clark, 1998.

Barth, Karl. *Church Dogmatics.* Vol. I/1. Edinburgh: T&T Clark, 1936.

Bauckham, Richard. *Jesus and the God of Israel: God Crucified and Other Studies on the New Testament's Christology of Divine Identity.* Grand Rapids, MI: Eerdmans, 2008.

Berkowitz, Ariel, and D'vorah Berkowitz. *Torah Rediscovered.* 5th ed. Shoreshim Publishing, inc, 2012.

Bird, Michael. *The Saving Righteousness of God: Studies on Paul, Justification and the New Perspective.* Wipf and Stock, 2007.

Blomberg, Craig L. *The Historical Reliability of the New Testament: Countering the Challenges to Evangelical Christian Belief.* Nashville, TN: B&H Academic, n.d.

Boteach, Shmuley. *Kosher Jesus.* Gefen Publishing House, 2012.

Brown, Michael L. *The Real Kosher Jesus.* Charisma Media, 2012.

Bultmann, Rudolph. *Primitive Christianity in Its Contemporary Setting*. New York, NY: Meridian Books, 1956.

Calvin, John. *Commentaries on the Epistle of Paul to the Philippians, Colossians, and Thessalonians*. Translated by John Pringle. Christian Classics Ethereal Library, https://ccel.org/ccel/calvin/calcom42/calcom42.i.html.

Carid, G.B. *Paul's Letters From Prison*. Oxford University Press, 1976.

Cha, M.I. *Misunderstanding Galatians: An Exegetical, Originalist Commentary*. Wipf and Stock, 2021.

Chamblin, Knox. "Law of Moses and the Law of Christ." In *Continuity and Discontinuity: Perspectives on the Relationship Between the Old and the New Testaments*. Edited by John S. Feinberg. Crossway, 1988.

Charles, R.H, ed. *The Letter of Aristeas*. The Clarendon Press, 1913. https://www.ccel.org/c/charles/otpseudepig/aristeas.htm.

Charlesworth, James H, ed. *The Old Testament Pseudepigrapha*. Vol. 2. Doubleday and Company, 1985.

Chesterton, G.K. "Enemies of Property." In *G.K. Chesterton Collected Works: Family, Society, Politics*. Vol. 4. Ignatius Press, 1987.

———. *The Everlasting Man*. London: Hodder and Stoughton, 1926.

Cobb, John B., and David Ray Griffin. *Process Theology: A Introductory Exposition*. Louisville, KY: Westminster John Knox Press, 1976.

Cohen, Shaye J.D. "Crossing the Boundary and Becoming a Jew." *Harvard Theological Review* 82, no. 1 (1989).

———. "The Origins of the Matrilineal Principle in Rabbinic Law." *AJS Review* 10, no. 1 (1985).

———. "Was Timothy Jewish? Acts 16:1-3." *JBL* 105, no. 2 (1986).

Collman, Ryan D. "(Un)Making a Theological Mountain Out of a Cardiological Mohel: Heart-Circumcision in Paul's Epistles." *JJMJS* 10 (2023).

Cranfield, C.E.B. *A Critical and Exegetical Commentary on the Epistle to the Romans.* Vol. 1 and 2. 2 vols. Edinburgh: T&T Clark, 1975.

Cullmann, Oscar. *The Earliest Christian Confessions.* Edited by Gary Habermas and Benjamin Charles Shaw. Translated by J.K.S. Reid. Wipf and Stock, 2018.

Davies, W.D. *Christian Origins and Judaism.* Arno Press, 1973.

Deissmann, Adolf. *Light from the Ancient East.* Grand Rapids, MI: Baker, 1978.

DeSilva, David A. *Honor, Patronage, Kinship, and Purity: Unlocking New Testament Culture.* IVP, 2022.

Dunn, D.G. *The Acts of the Apostles.* Trinity Press International, 1996.

———. *The Epistle to the Galatians.* Edited by Henry Chadwick. Black's New Testament Commentary. Eerdmans, 1996.

Ehrman, Bart D. *The Apostolic Fathers: Clement. II Clement. Ignatius. Polycarp. Didache.* Vol. 1.1. Harvard University Press, 2003.

Fruchtenbaum, Arnold G. *Israelology: The Missing Link in Systematic Theology.* San Antonio, TX: Ariel Ministries, 2016.

Geiermann, Peter. *Convert's Catechism of Catholic Doctrine.* 12th ed. St. Louis, MO: B. Herder, 1937. https://curate.nd.edu/downloads/und:bv73bz63h5c.

Goddard, A.J., and S.A. Cummins. "Ill or Ill-Treated? Conflict and Persecution as the Context of Paul's Original Ministry in Galatia (Galatians 4:12-20)." *Journal for the Study of the New Testament* 52 (1993).

Hall, Robert G. "Epispasm: Circumcision in Reverse." *Bible Review,* 1992.

Hartshorne, Charles. *Divine Relativity*. New Haven, CT: Yale University Press, 1982.

Hegg, Tim. *A Commentary on the Epistle to the Ephesians*. Torah Resource, 2019.

———. "All Things to All Men: Paul and the Torah in 1 Cor. 9:19-23." *Torah Resource*, n.d. https://torahresource.com/all-things-to-all-men/.

———. "Can We Speak of 'Law' in the New Testament in Monolithic Terms." *Northwest Region Meeting*, 1995.

———. *Paul's Epistle to the Galatians*. 2nd ed. Tacoma, WA: Torah Resource, 2010.

———. "The Chronology of the Crucifixion: A Comparison of the Gospel Accounts." *Torah Resource*, 2017.

———. *The Letter Writer: Paul's Background and Torah Perspective*. 2nd ed. Tacoma, WA: Torah Resource, 2008.

Heye, Bekele. *Sabbath in Ethiopia: An Exploration of Christian Roots*. Center for Creative Ministry, 2003.

Hoehner, Harold W. *Ephesians: An Exegetical Commentary*. Baker Academic, 2002.

Horner, David A. "Aut Deus Aut Malus Homo: A Defense of C.S. Lewis's 'Shocking Alternative.'" In *C.S. Lewis as Philosopher Truth, Goodness, and Beauty*. 2nd ed. Lynchburg, VA: Liberty University Press, 2017.

Jacob, Alex. *The Case for Enlargement Theology*. Glory to Glory Publications, 2011.

Jeremias, Joachim. *The Eucharistic Words of Jesus*. Macmillin, 1955.

Johnson, Luke Timothy. *The Acts of the Apostles*. Edited by Daniel J. Harrington. Liturgical Press, 1992.

Keener, Craig S. *Acts: An Exegetical Commentary*. Vol. 3. Baker Academic, 2014.

———. *Galatians: A Commentary.* Baker Academic, 2019.

———. *Miracles: The Credibility of the New Testament Accounts.* Grand Rapids, MI: Baker, 2012.

King, Barbra. *Evolving God: A Provocative View on the Origins of Religion.* Chicago, IL: University of Chicago Press, 2017.

Kinzer, Mark. *Post-Missionary Messianic Judaism: Redefining Christian Engagement with the Jewish People.* Brazos, 2005.

Koelner, Yosef, and Jeffery Seif. *Sha'ul/Paul God's Shaliach (Apostle) Corresponds with the Corinthians.* Messianic Jewish Publishers, 2023.

Laansma, J.C. "The Lord's Day." In *The Dictionary of the Later New Testament and Its Developments.* IVP, 1997.

Lancaster, Thomas D. *From Sabbath to Sabbath: Returning the Holy Sabbath to the Disciples of Jesus.* First Fruits of Zion, 2016.

———. *The Holy Epistle to the Galatians.* First Fruits of Zion, 2011.

Lewis, C.S. "Christian Apologetics." In *God in the Dock.* Edited by Walter Hooper. Grand Rapids, MI: Eerdmans, 2001.

———. *Mere Christianity.* New York, NY: Harper Collins, 2001.

———. "Rejoinder to Dr. Pittenger." In *God in the Dock.* Edited by Walter Hooper. Grand Rapids, MI: Eerdmans, 2001.

———. *The Lion, the Witch and the Wardrobe.* New York, NY: Harper Collins, 2001.

———. *Voyage of the Dawn Treader.* New York, NY: Harper Collins, 1994.

———. "What Are We to Make of Jesus Christ." In *God in the Dock.* Edited by Walter Hooper. Grand Rapids, MI: Eerdmans, 2001.

Lightfoot, J.B. *St. Paul's Epistle to the Galatians.* Warren Draper, 1870.

Lindbeck, George A. *The Nature of Doctrine: Religion and Theology in a Post-Liberal Age.* Louisville, KY: Westminster John Knox Press, 2009.

Longenecker, Richard N. *Galatians*. Edited by Bruce M. Metzger. World Biblical Commentary 41. Word, 1990.

Marguerat, Daniel. *Paul in Acts and Paul in His Letters*. Mohr Siebeck, 2013.

McArthur, John. "Why Sunday Is the Lord's Day." https://www.gty.org/library/sermons-library/90-380/-/about.

McKee, J.K. *The New Testament Validates Torah*. Messianic Apologetics, 2012.

McKenzie, Gregory S. "In the Wake of Euthyphro's False Dilemma." *Elutheria* 5, no. 2 (December 2021).

———. "Pronomian Paradigm: A Pro-Torah, Christocentric Method for Theology and Apologetics." PhD Dissertation, Liberty University, 2024.

Metzger, Bruce M. *Apocrypha of the Old Testament*. Oxford University Press, 1977.

———. *The Saturday and Sunday Lessons from Luke in the Greek Gospel Lectionary, Studies in the Lectionary Text of the Greek New Testament*. Vol. 2. Chicago University Press, 1944.

Montegiore, C.G., and H.M.J. Loewe, eds. *A Rabbinic Anthology*. Cambridge University Press, 2012.

Moo, Douglas. *Pillar New Testament Commentary: The Letter to the Colossians and to Philemon*. Eerdmans, 2008.

Mordechai, Avi Ben. *Galatians: A Torah Based Commentary in First-Century Hebraic Context*. Millennium 7000 Communication, 2005.

Morrison, John Douglas. *Has God Said?, The Word of God, and the Crisis of Theological Authority*. Eugene, OR: Pickwick Publications, 2006.

Nanos, Mark. "Paul's Non-Jews Do Not Become 'Jews' But Do They Become 'Jewish'? Reading Romans 2:25-29 Within Judaism, Alongside Josephus." *JJMJS* 1 (2014).

———. *The Irony of Galatians*. Portland, OR: Fortress Press, 2002.

———. *The Mystery of Romans: The Jewish Context of Paul's Letters*. Minneapolis, MN: Fortress Press, 1996.

Newsom, Carol. *Songs of the Sabbath Sacrifice: A Critical Edition*. Vol. 27. Harvard Semitic Studies. Brill, 1985.

Oakes, Karl R. *From Torah to Paul: The Prehistory of the Catholic Church*. Wipf and Stock, 2016.

O'Brien, Peter T. *Word Biblical Commentary: Colossians, Philemon*. Thomas Nelson, 1982.

Oswalt, John N. *The Bible Among the Myths*. Grand Rapids, MI: Zondervan, 2009.

Persaud, Raj, and Peter Bruggen. "Can You Lose Your Eyesight for Psychological Reasons." *Psychology Today*, August 17, 2015. https://www.psychologytoday.com/us/blog/slightly-blighty/201508/can-you-lose-your-eyesight-psychological-reasons.

Polhill, John B. *Acts*. Vol. 26. The New American Commentary. Broadman and Holman, 1992.

Pritz, Ray A. *Nazarene Jewish Christianity: From the End of the New Testament Period Until Its Disappearance in the Fourth Century*. Jerusalem: Magnes Press, 1992.

Rabbinowitz, Noel S. "Matthew 23:2-4: Does Jesus Recognize the Authority of the Pharisees and Does He Endorse Their Halakah?" *Journal of the Evangelical Theological Society* 46, no. 3 (2003).

Robertson, O. Palmer. *The Flow of the Psalms: Discovering Their Structure and Theology*. Phillipsburg, NJ: Presbyterian and Reformed Publishing Company, 2015.

Rosner, Brian S., and Roy E. Ciampa. *First Letter to the Corinthians.* Apollos, 2010.

Rushdoony, Rousas John. *Leviticus.* Vol. 3rd Commentaries on the Pentateuch. Vallecito, CA: Ross House Books, 2005.

Ryrie, Charles C. *Basic Theology.* Victor Books, 1986.

———. *Dispensationalism.* Chicago, IL: Moody Press, 2007.

Sanders, E.P. *Judaism: Practice and Belief 63BCE-66CE.* Trinity Press International, 1992.

———. *Paul, the Law, and the Jewish People.* Minneapolis, MN: Fortress Press, 1977.

Savelle, Charles. "Acts 15:21: Moses Is Preached and Read in the Synagogues." *JETS* 65, no. 4 (2022).

Schofield, C.I. *Scofield Reference Bible.* Oxford University Press, 1909.

Silva, Moises. *Interpreting Galatians.* Baker, 2001.

Staples, Jason A. "Altered Because of Transgressions? The 'Law of Deeds' in Gal. 3.19a." *Zeitschrift Fur Die Neutestamentliche Wissenschaft* 106, no. 1 (2015).

———. *Paul and the Resurrection of Israel: Jews, Former Gentiles, Israelites.* Cambridge University Press, 2024.

Stendahl, Krister. "The Apostle Paul and the Introspective Conscience of the West." *Harvard Theological Review* 56, no. 3 (n.d.).

Stern, David H. *Jewish New Testament Commentary.* Clarksville, MD: Jewish New Testament Publications, 1996.

Szumskyj, Benjamin. "The Role of the Law in the Sanctification of the Believer Today: A Brief Introduction to Pronomianism." PhD Dissertation, Liberty University, 2024.

Tenney, Merrill C. *New Testament Survey Revised.* Edited by Walter M Dunnett. Grand Rapids, MI: Eerdmans, 1985.

Thiessen, Matthew. *Contesting Conversion.* Oxford University Press, 2011.

————. *The Gentile Problem*. Oxford University Press, 2016.

Vanhoff, Rob. "Circumcision in the Second Temple Period: Part 3." *Torah Resource*, 2012.

Wallace, Daniel B. *Greek Grammar: Beyond the Basics: An Exegetical Syntax of the New Testament*. Zondervan, 1997.

Warfield, Benjamin B. *The Inspiration and Authority of the Bible*. Edited by Samuel G. Craig. Phillipsburg, NJ: Presbyterian and Reformed Publishing Company, 1948.

Whitehead, Alfred. *Process and Reality: An Essay in Cosmology*. Edited by David Ray Griffin and Donald W. Sherburne. New York, NY: The Free Press, 1978.

Wilber, David. *How Jesus Fulfilled the Law: A Pronomian Pocket Guide to Matthew 5:17-20*. Pronomian Publishing, 2024.

————. *Remember the Sabbath: What the New Testament Says About Sabbath Observance for Christians*. Pronomian Publishing, 2022.

Williams, Logan, and Paul T. Sloan. "Neither Sabbath nor Kashrut, but a Demonic Third Thing: Pagan Holidays and Food Sacrificed to Idols in Romans 14:1-23." San Antonio, TX, 2023.

Witherington III, Ben. *The Acts of the Apostles*. Eerdmans, 1998.

Wright, N.T. *Justification: God's Plan and Paul's Vision*. IVP Academic, 2009.

————. *Paul and the Faithfulness of God*. Fortress Press, 2013.

Yarhouse, Mark A. Understanding Gender Dysphoria: Navigating Transgender Issues in a Changing Culture. Downers Grove, IL: Intervarsity, 2015.

Zenger, Erich. *A God of Vengeance: Understanding the Psalms of Divine Wrath*. Translated by Linda M. Maloney. Louisville, KY: Westminster John Knox Press, 1994.

www.ingramcontent.com/pod-product-compliance
Lightning Source LLC
Chambersburg PA
CBHW060323050426
42449CB00011B/2626